PHILIP LARKIN, THE MARVELL PRESS AND ME

D1354141

PHILIP LARKIN,
THE MARVELL PRESS
AND ME

JEAN HARTLEY

faber and faber

This edition first published in 2010
by Faber and Faber Ltd
Bloomsbury House, 74–77 Great Russell Street
London WC1B 3DA

Printed by CPI Antony Rowe, Eastbourne

A CIP record for this book is available from the British Library

ISBN 978-0-571-26990-7

For Laurien and Alison

Acknowledgements

The trustees of the estate of Philip Larkin have been good enough to allow me to reprint the various letters and cards from Philip Larkin. Barbara Watson gave me permission to quote from one of Joan Barton's letters and the estate of John Betjeman has allowed me to print quotations from two of John Betjeman's letters.

I should like to thank the following people for their help and advice: Charles Brook, Brian Dyson, the University's Archivist, Iris Carlin, Jill Carter, Pam Flynn, Daphne and Peter Glazer, Chris Goss, Alison Hartley, Harry Holland, Laurien Holland, Victor Holland, Christopher Ketchell, Joyce and Steve Ramsey, Jyotirmaya Sharma, Noel and Margot O'Sullivan, Marion Shaw and Madge Turner.

I am especially grateful to Maeve Brennan for allowing me to quote from the tribute to Philip Larkin that she delivered on the Memorial Evening at Hull University. She also helped me with various details and dates that I was unsure of.

Rob Watkinson gave me good advice and made many useful suggestions as did Frank Redpath, who also helped me to recall so many events in which he was involved.

I am indebted to Ted Tarling for letting me reprint Philip's letters to him, and for his invaluable assistance.

Peter Wilkes spent many hours cleaning, copying and enlarging my collection of old photographs. Throughout the preparation of the book he gave me support, encouragement and advice.

Illustrations

One

I was born in the heart of Hull's fishing community and my earliest recollection is of a grey, littered street swarming with children and noisy with the clamour of their street games: at dinner-time, and after school, they bowled bicycle-wheels, chalked out hopscotches on the pavements, played chasing games and some of the luckier kids staggered high on wooden stilts or sped up and down on roller skates. Terraces of twelve houses intersected the street at regular intervals: ours was called Ivy Terrace.

As soon as the men had gone to work in the mornings, the women in pinafores, with infants clinging to their legs, would appear in the terrace to shake mats, lean on brooms or stand with arms akimbo, and the morning gossip would begin. I would view this activity from my vantage point behind the front-room net curtains, for my mother, though she was neighbourly, was not one of the throng. She fancied herself a cut above the others, having been in service with a gentleman's family before she married, and she tried to bring a measure of that gentility to her own mean household. When going out for even the briefest of shopping trips, she dressed in a smart two-piece suit and hat, both of which she had made. At the Alderman Cogan Charity School for Poor Girls she had received a good grounding in domestic economy, but she had picked up for herself the more sophisticated skills.

My dad, a stocky, bowlegged man with cauliflower ears, a broken nose (he had been a keen street-corner boxer in his teens) and piercingly honest blue eyes, was already ill by the time I was born. Proud of his strength and haunted by the spectre of unemployment, as a young man he had taken a labouring job in the foundry of the marine engineering firm of Charles D. Holmes. The regular wage kept the family afloat but working in the intense heat and fumes soon ruined his health; the most regular noise in our house was the sound of my father's wheezing, coughing and spitting. Billy Holland was adored by everyone who knew him. Grindingly poor though we were, he would always spare a little money or buy a bag of groceries for a workmate who was worse off than we. Newly-wed friends received an expertly hand-crafted poker, shovel and brass nut-crackers moulded in the shape of a woman's nether half (raw materials by unwitting courtesy of C. D. Holmes – as was most of our firewood, though the latter was more in my brother's line). My father had 'spoken for' Harry, who was nine years older than me, and had got him an apprenticeship as a wood pattern-maker, the most skilled and prestigious job in the wood-working field. 'Harry works to a thousandth of an inch' was the proud boast in our family.

One day, coming back from shopping on the teeming main road, my mother and I noticed a knot of people gathered at the top of the terrace. On going nearer we saw a fisherman in wide-bottomed trousers – a great ape of a man – holding a red-haired neighbour of ours by the throat and banging her head against the wall. Her choking sobs could be heard over his foul imprecations and I clutched my mother's arm and whispered, 'Can't somebody stop him?' 'No', she said. 'You can't interfere between man and wife. He always knocks her about when he comes home from sea.' This kind of public domestic violence and the after-closing-time street-fight outside the pub were commonplace in the 1930s.

For some months there had been a teasing preparation by my brother for my first day at school. Here it was, a warm May morning, sun on the dirty street, groups of un-shaven, hard-eyed men standing about (this was 1938), and me in a new red velvet dress that mother had made.

I didn't like school. It was an ugly, red-brick, Victorian monster with white tiled classrooms and smelly lavatories, but worst of all was the crowd in the playground. The noise was shrill and deafening and wherever you stood someone would rush past or bang into you. So I decided not to go to school any more. I told my mother at lunch time and she just pursed her lips. All seemed to be settled until she grabbed my arm and said 'Come on, Milady, back you go.'

Of course I resisted and sobbed and sat down on the pavement and screamed. People ran out of their houses to see what the trouble was and shouted advice to my mother: 'Give her a good hiding', 'Lock her in a dark cup-board' and so on. After dragging me three hundred yards on my bottom, she won. I stood in the classroom, my face now dirty except for the tear channels and my lovely red dress dusty and smeared. All right, I said to myself as the other infants gawped at me in wonder. They've got me here but they can't stop me hating it. School, for me, was a cornucopia of shame and humiliation. A year later I com-mitted some minor misdemeanour, perhaps talking, and was called up to the teacher's desk. After giving me a good rousting she ordered me to apologize. I looked at her blankly. 'Apologize!' she repeated over and over and, re-ceiving no reply, she whacked my hand with a wooden ruler until the ruler broke in half. Smarting with pain and outrage, I ran home to my mother and asked, 'What does apologize mean?' How many working-class children, I wonder, are punished for being dumbly insolent when in fact they are simply too scared to show their ignorance?

My brother was, for a time, what I believe is called a shifted sinistral, though not from choice. When it was dis-covered that he was left-handed, Mr Peacock, his teacher, told him to change hands. Since the desks were double-

11

barrelled, he claimed that Harry's writing position hampered the calligraphy of his partner. Harry made efforts, became absorbed in his work, forgot, and changed back to doing what came naturally. The sharp-eyed Mr Peacock declared it was the school's policy that all children should write with their right hands, so he forcibly tied Harry's left one behind his back until the problem was cured.

My senior school was no better. The tortoise-faced maths teacher must have had secret yearnings to join the ATS for her clothes – even her underskirt and knee-length bloomers – were all khaki coloured. She wrote the sums on the backboard and then crept round the desks in her crepe-soled sandals. When she saw that I had made a mistake she thumped me on the back. The jolt shot the ink off the nib of my dip-pen and produced a blot. Next time she came round she thumped me again for having blotted my book. Four years with khaki Miss Clark ensured my hopelessness at maths. My only talent was for English, taught by the sweet-faced Miss Senior. She fostered my love of poetry and lent me books of her own to take home.

As soon as war was declared, I was evacuated to Filey, a small East Coast town about forty miles from Hull. For a six-year-old, going to live at the seaside should have been exciting but it was not. My visions of sand-castles, paddling and ice-cream cornets were quickly dispelled by the sight of the barbed-wire fence that cordoned off the beach. I cannot remember much about my months at Filey apart from feeling miserable, lonely and withdrawn. I had gone from being the much-cherished youngest member of a small family to being the unconsidered youngest member of a much-extended household. The fisherman and his wife that I was billeted with were stern, angular, hard-worked folk with two children of their own as well as three other billettees – a married woman from Hull with her two children. Consequently, I got short shrift.

At Christmas my parents sent me a selection box of chocolates which must have represented an enormous saving-up of sweet coupons. I saw the box arrive, was allowed to admire it and then it was put away, never to reappear. I was worried secretly about the luscious chocolate bars and brooded over the loss of them. Perhaps they would be brought out the next day, or the next week? But no. I had not the nerve to ask the forbidding adults what had happened to them. Instead I used my initiative and sent a postcard to my parents saying that I did not like being in Filey and that I wanted to come back to Hull. It seemed to my parents a good suggestion at the time; during those months of 'the phoney war', the expected bombardment had not come and all at home was peaceful.

Our house was a hive of industry. My mother baked twice a week (brown bread on Tuesdays, white on Fridays) and always made an extra half dozen small loaves which she and I took round in a basket covered with a clean tea-towel to various 'poor persons', one of whom was my father's stepmother, a frail old lady who was lumbered with a number of middle-aged ne'er-do-well sons. They appeared half-dressed and bed-rumpled in socks, longjohns and unbuttoned grandad shirts in the middle of the afternoon, to pounce on the newly-baked bread. As young soldiers in the First World War the death and destruction they witnessed had turned them into hard boozers. Returning home, masters of no trade, to a town where the unemployment rate was always high, they had drifted into jobs as draymen and casual labourers.

Fecklessness was not encouraged in our house and, looking back, our existence was a miracle of make-do-and-mend and the sort of recycling that would gladden the heart of a present-day ecologist. *The Daily Herald* and *John Bull* (a bit shiny, this) were torn into neat squares and hung on a hook in the lavatory. Harry monopolized the kitchen table to make out of discarded bed-ends or old wardrobe doors his fiendishly accurate scale models of Spitfires and Heinkels. Dad had a last on which, with worn-out bits of belting from the machines at work, he mended our shoes and then banged metal segs into the toes and heels to make

13

them last longer. In winter we all helped my mother to make brightly-coloured rag rugs, ready to replace the old ones in spring – they were immensely difficult to clean. Gathered round the fire, we snipped up old coats and skirts into four-inch lengths and pricked them into a sacking base while we listened to Saturday Night Theatre or roared with laughter over *ITMA* or *Happydrome*.

Boyes, an old-fashioned store at the corner of the street, used to sell off bankrupt stock and hold Fire Sales of material that had been damaged or discoloured by the water used to put out the blaze. Mum would buy the stuff, wash it, make it into pillow-cases to sell back to Boyes and make Harry a cricket shirt out of the remnants. He wore many a pair of trousers that had once been a navy-blue skirt, unpicked and turned to show the unfaded side. 'Waste not want not' was my mother's dictum, but sometimes her thrift went too far. I remember being cut almost to ribbons by the knickers she made for me out of a bargain length of sailcloth.

My first meeting with members of the middle class took place during the war, in the street's communal air-raid shelter at the top of the small avenue of six houses down which we now lived. (We had 'flitted' from a neighbouring street to this one in 1940. Only the affluent could afford a removal van and, in any case, no one in our circumstances had enough household goods to warrant one. Dad hired a handcart, sixpence for the night, and in half a dozen journeys he and Harry had completed the move.) Miss Jackson and her uncle lived in the big house across the road. At the beginning of the century, the tree-lined Boulevard was occupied by rich merchants, ships' captains, doctors and dentists, who later moved out to the town's suburbs. These houses had ornately plastered ceilings and wooden porches decorated with intricate bits of woodcarving. Our little avenue of two-up-and-two-downs had been built to accommodate the servants who would work in the big houses on a daily basis.

14

Plump and middle-aged Miss Jackson managed a sweet-shop by day and played the violin in the Hull Philharmonic Orchestra at night. Uncle was a little old man, retired from the haberdashery business. He wore a velvet smoking-jacket and a trilby hat over a knitted balaclava to keep the night air from his bald head or 'flies' playground' as my brother irreverently called it. Uncle had no time for the military and referred to them scathingly as 'brasshats and tinswords'. He and his niece came into the shelter clutching important-looking deed boxes. My mother carried a zip-up bag containing insurance policies, birth certificates, her marriage lines and her knitting.

We trickled into the shelter from about 10 p.m onwards (if the air-raid warning siren had not sent us scuttling in before), after having eaten our bread and jam supper, listened to the nine o'clock news and locked up the house. Each of us carried a gasmask, an ex-army blanket and a pillow and we stayed in the shelter until about 6 a.m when we deemed ourselves safe from the predations of the *Luftwaffe*. Most of the shelter's occupants were women, the very old or the very young. My mother's gentility endeared us to Miss Jackson and Uncle and a bargain was struck over the sweet coupons. We handed ours over to Miss Jackson and in return she let us buy the best – Roses chocolates and Quality Street – and she threw in an off-the-ration buckshee quarter of Mintoes. Through the night we would shuffle to get comfortable on the wooden benches, re-plumping the pillow to get some softness between the head and the brick wall.

We looked ghostly when we emerged in the grey dawn – drowsy figures quietly stealing back to our houses with arms full of bedding and a thin feeling of relief at having lived through another night. There were few nights when the shelter was not shaken by the blast from bomb explosions in neighbouring streets or further down our own. The fish-and-chip shop fifty yards from us was hit by the blast from a landmine one night before closing time. The whole queue and the proprietors were killed instantly.

My brother had just called in there for his fry when it happened. He arrived home as Mum, Dad and I were eating our supper and listening to the radio. We were having a rare treat that night, as Mother had opened a tin of Australian greengage jam and decanted it into a basin. As I leaned forward to spread some on my bread and marge there was an almighty crash, the lights went out and the radio was silenced. We fumbled through glass, wood and masonry to find the torch and some candles. Our main fear was for my father, whose chair was in front of the blacked-out window. The torch's thin beam revealed him struggling and cursing his way out of the window-frame which hung round his neck. Fortunately, the thick curtains had protected his head and shoulders from the avalanche of glass that had descended on him. We picked our way through the debris in order to size up the rest of the damage. The blast had wrenched the front door off its hinges and blown it clean up the stairs and on to the landing. No window remained intact and every piece of furniture in the house was pitted and scratched. I was taken away from the blazing street down dark alleyways to stay with my Aunt Madge while Mum, Dad and Harry boarded up the windows and fixed the doors. This was the first thing to be done, otherwise looters might walk in and lift all the household goods. Within three days the house had been made reasonably habitable. It was nearly forty years before the fish-shop bomb site was properly levelled and planted with a few shrubs and saplings.

At my aunt's I was sardined into a single bed with my young cousins. I cried quietly to myself at the shock of it all and grieved over the greengage jam that I had not tasted and that was, when last seen, covered in soot and shards of glass.

By 1943 I was evacuated to Lincolnshire and my father had been drafted into the RASC. My mother and brother remained in Hull. Harry, who was fascinated by ships and aeroplanes, longed to join the RAF but he was not allowed to do so for he was in a reserved occupation, helping to build minesweepers. Knowledge of this did not prevent a few ill-intentioned folk from sending white feathers to my mother.

My brother worked in atrocious conditions in a badly-lit pattern shop, making from blueprints the wooden proto- types of parts that were to be cast into metal. He worked from 7.30 a.m. to 8 p.m. each week day and until dinner time on Saturdays. One night a week he did Home Guard duty at Costello Park where he helped to man the big anti- aircraft guns. Like the majority of people, he was ex- hausted, underfed, had one threadbare suit of clothes to his name, and felt low-spirited. He refused to spend any more comfortless nights in the air-raid shelter, and told my mother that if he were to die he would prefer to die in his own bed.

Two

At the age of nine, with a dozen or so other children, I was herded on to the New Holland Packet, the steamer which made daily crossings of the River Humber. With gas-mask cases slung on our shoulders and identity discs round our necks, we were taken from our blitzed homes to a tiny village in Lincolnshire. Once there we sat cross-legged on the green for the village ladies to size us up and make their choice. The Major's wife, a hawk-faced woman who wore bright make-up, country tweeds and two-tone court shoes, selected me – because I looked clean, she said. I was given a pleasant little room to sleep in but in the daytime I was kept in the kitchen, with the maid, to help her with the chores. One day when the family was out, I answered the telephone and when they returned I relayed the message. The fact that I had the gumption to take messages was marvelled over for days. I was not happy there. The house rang with haughty upper-class voices and the one-eyed major and his tall, be-jodphured sons strutted about carrying riding-crops, but the maid was kind and she showed me how to make Marmite and cucumber sandwiches which, nearly half a century later, I still enjoy.

My stay there was brief. One day the Major's wife had detailed me to clean her bedroom. Lacking the necessary expertise, I had a quick flick round with the duster then, easing the shoe-trees out of her two-tone courts, and making my mouth into a cupid's bow with her orange lipstick, I did a clumsy dance in front of the mirror (my mum wore no cosmetics, no bra and only the most serviceable shoes so, to me, this was film star territory). Through the mirror I saw the Major's wife come through the door, her face purple with fury and outrage. That night I wet my bed. Next day, when it was discovered, there were further stormy scenes in the kitchen culminating in the threat, 'If you wet the bed again you'll have to go.' And, of course, I did.

I do not know how I came to be in my next billet. Perhaps the working-class Towles had advertised for an incipient bed-wetter, but it is more likely that the lady of the manor's directive was law. The middle-aged couple made me very welcome and treated me as one of the family. When their nineteen-year-old daughter, Chrissie, came home on leave from the WAAF, I fell in love with her. She was not beautiful, though to me, feeling displaced, ugly and oozing self-pity, she seemed so with her thick yellow hair, ripe figure and roguish smile. She had a fine voice and it was a joy to hear her singing 'Yours till the stars lose their glory' or 'Perfidia' as she helped with the housework.

The war seemed to have passed the village by except that the outskirts on three sides of it were occupied by Italian POW's, the British Air Force and the American Army respectively. 'Got any gum, chum', we shouted to the latter as they drawled past us in their beautifully tailored uniforms. But we seldom heard the zoom of aircraft and never the screech and thud of bombs – a recurring nightmare of mine since the night we just missed the land-mine.

The next time Chrissie came home on leave there were great celebrations and lots of talk about the forthcoming wedding. I do not know why she wanted to marry the silent and unsmiling Eddie Bowles but I gathered there had been an 'understanding' ever since they left school and I suppose at that time Chrissie had not thought of widening her horizons. Eddie was a paratrooper and I was quite sure he must have been the inventor of the barbaric ritual of drubbing – a torture practised by the big boys in the school – which consisted of making a fist and rubbing the taut knuckles hard on the heads of girls and smaller boys after having secured the services of an accomplice to hold the victims down. I dreaded playtime every day I was at the village school. My hatred of Eddie stemmed from the day when he refused to let me look at his cigarette lighter. Later that morning we all went into the snowy paddock, which lay in front of the Towles' house, and played snowballs. Suddenly he began chasing me and, after a struggle, he pushed me down and started shovelling snow on top of me with both hands. Chrissie shouted to him to stop. I was hysterical and could not breathe. Perhaps the fact that I was timid and a poor sport goaded him to carry on. Eventually, of course, he stopped, dug me out and helped me up but I never liked him or his thin-lipped face after that. Later I heard someone say he was neurotic and I clung to the word. To be able to pin such a medical sounding term on Eddie seemed like a good way of getting even with him.

When their leave was up, Chrissie and Eddie went back to their units and the old, stone-built dower house seemed very quiet and empty. Mr Towle, a bricklayer, took his toolbag and went out to work every morning at seven on his sit-up-and-beg bike, across the paddock and then God knows where. At nine o'clock he came back for his breakfast of bacon, egg and fried potatoes (this meal alone would have been a banquet for the majority of tightly-rationed town dwellers). The three of us would eat, Mr Towle occasionally looking up from his morning paper to make a joke, often at my expense. They were not unkindly people but I was a testing ground for their measure of how dumb a city child could be. Half the time, I only pretended to be ignorant, ill-informed and naïve to please them. It seemed an indulgence and I expected them to divine that really all this was just a game. Perhaps I expected too much of them: the simplicity of their lives would not have accustomed them to the idea of manipulating reality by imaginative role-playing. In any case, I realize now that much of our misunderstanding stemmed from a language problem, and the impatience each of us felt with the other's accent and dialect.

Looking back, my days seem to have been spent in the surrounding copses and lanes, hunting for wild violets, primroses and snowdrops. School does not bring back many memories, apart from the morning assembly when we sang (surely not every day) 'New every morning is the love'. I doubt if we learned very much since all ages were taught in the one classroom. There were the usual tensions and minor scandals. Nellie from the fens arrived one morning with streaky blonde hair. (The fen people were an alien breed with their own mysterious culture.) All eyes were riveted to this hair, which had been black the day before, and at playtime we all besieged her with questions, to which she would only answer 'Mum washed it in Persil'. Another day, during the afternoon lessons, we heard loud thwacking noises issuing from the Headmaster's study. Jimmy, a thirteen-year-old, came out a few minutes later looking pained but unbowed. His crime had been to urinate in a milk bottle and place it on the teacher's desk. This, for some reason, increased his prestige with the older pupils but we young ones were horrified.

Spring came. The horse-chestnut tree on the village green, said to be one of the oldest in England, started budding, and my mother sent me a white dress with a shawl collar edged with lace. I thought it the most exquisite thing in the world and then was alarmed to learn I would be wearing it when I presented Chrissie with a horseshoe at her wedding. (Adults arrange things behind your back.) I was torn between suppressed excitement and gloom. My nose, I had long suspected and now confirmed, was at least three-quarters of an inch bigger than it ought to be, my elbows were red and my hair hung lank. Oh, everyone must despise me; how ridiculous I would look.

The aunts began to descend from surrounding villages. Large and bellicose in maroon crêpe-de-Chine, thin and desiccated in navy marocain, they stuffed chines, whipped cream, concocted monstrous trifles, talked about how their stays hurt and generally prepared for the wedding. I was kept busy running errands to nearby houses and farms to deliver coded messages. I returned bearing secret packages of butter, cheese and other black-market items: 'Remember to go to the back door and don't let anybody see you.' On the last day I was sent to the Hall for some sprigs of orange-blossom. At first I thought this was another joke like elbow grease or skyhooks, but I loved the sound of it and hoped it was not. The Hall was a square, three-storeyed mansion occupied by a tough spinster with salt-and-pepper hair and trousers. I had seen her in the village with four dogs on leashes, admonishing them in her husky Craven A voice. A cigarette usually hung from one side of her mouth and she often used the word 'bloody'. A maid in uniform opened the door at the tradesman's entrance and scurried round to the back garden. Soon she returned with orange-blossom, an armful of it, and the sweet smell of the white flowers brought a lump to my throat.

At the wedding feast I had to sit with Lena, Eddie's daft sister with whom, ever since the engagement, I had been expected to play in order, perhaps, to strengthen the union between the two families. Maybe the friendship was imposed because Lena was shunned by all the other children on account of her long blank face and vacant eyes. No less cruel than the rest, I finally lost patience and kicked her when she refused, out of timidity I thought but perhaps it was family loyalty, to help me steal plums from her mother's tree.

Three weeks later my mother wrote to say the air raids had eased off and to ask if I would like to come home for a while. The general feeling of post-nuptial anti-climax and adult irritation helped me to make up my mind, but mother had been premature in thinking the raids were over. Within a week of my return they began again.

Despite his chronic bronchitis, a legacy from the years of hard graft in the iron foundry, my father, aged forty-two, had been called up when the War Office was reduced to taking in Grade C men. He spent the remainder of the war aggravating his chest condition in wet tents in Ireland. I missed his big voice booming out 'Underneath the Arches' or some other music-hall favourite, and the house seemed empty without his cheery presence. Harry lived for Sundays when, whatever the weather, he would cycle into the country for a quiet day's fishing. My four-foot-something mother treadled the old Singer sewing-machine, dolly-tubbed our clothes and waited in endless food queues to buy our meagre rations. In the barn-like Co-op., our tiny portions were weighed out and parcelled up in blue sugar paper or greaseproof by the tall manager who had two or three long strands of hair pasted over his bald dome. I lived in a more glamorous world, revealed to me by my thrice-weekly visits to the cinema. My heroes did not lack hair nor were my heroines ever short of stockings. After tea, Mum and I devoured vast quantities of romantic fiction. Too busy during the day to slip next door and choose her own books from the Boulevard Branch Library, she would send me to ask for 'Two books for a lady, please.'

My school lessons were punctuated by gas-mask drill and we were not the most alert of pupils after a few hours of fitful sleep snatched in the air-raid shelter or the gas cupboard. After the raids there was a harvest of shrapnel to be gathered for doing swaps or just gloating over. It came in intriguing sizes and shapes, its texture jagged or smooth. After I had grown up and seen some modern sculpture, I was reminded of these 'found objects' and I wondered where all the shrapnel collections had gone.

The raids were becoming more intense, so I travelled back to Lincolnshire and was looking forward to this stay.

After Hull, twisted and torn and bomb-scarred, with loo-ters stealing even from occupied houses, the country seemed like a benediction. Chrissie had left the WAAF on the birth of Morris – a peevish, spoilt, pasty-faced child whom I pinched every time he shrieked when I was in charge of him. I got on Mrs Towle's nerves, which were never very strong (legend had it that she was run over by a motor car in her youth), by continually humming under my breath. What I lacked was books, but I do not remem-ber ever seeing any in that house apart from the Bible, and, what they called books: *Woman's Weekly* and odd copies of the parish magazine.

A great change came over the house after Chrissie got to know three Americans who lived in the Nissen huts in the Hall grounds. The way to the Hall and grounds was round the village green, past the schoolhouse and the church opposite and then down a leafy lane. But there was a quicker way for us; we walked down our garden, past the earth lavatory, the vegetable plot, fruit bushes and pig-sty and through a hole in the garden wall. It opened on to a very thick copse, full of birds and small, scurrying animals and after threading your way through this – there was no path – you came out into a clearing in the grounds. Often we would be sitting at the dining-table, gazing out into the garden, and see one of our American friends pop through the hole in the wall.

The one Chrissie loved was called Leo Wagner, a dentist in civvy street. He was genial, under medium height, over medium weight, had beautiful black wavy hair, strong black eyebrows and he always brought a cardboard box labelled 'delicatessen' whenever he came to the house. His friend, Franz, also a dentist and similar in appearance to Leo (except that his smile was not quite so winning), was in love with Joanna, a US army nurse whom I placed on a pedestal along with my favourite film stars of the day. Not only did she look like Linda Darnell, she also taught us how to make clam chowder.

Feeling homesick, they spent a lot of time at our house and Mrs Towle liked them to come because she was hospitable and fond of company. They joked and flattered her and, of course, brought lots of lovely food, the like of which was unobtainable except in US officers' messes. We grew our own fruit and vegetables and killed a pig from time to time, but the Americans brought strange delicacies, sweets galore and rich fruit-cakes stuffed with cherries, angelica, candied peel and nuts. However, I sensed a slight unease in Mrs Towle after these visits and vaguely traced it to the fact that Chrissie liked Leo and Franz liked Joanna but all four were married to different people.

Gone was the photograph of Eddie which had stood on Chrissie's dressing-table, and in its place was a much more professionally accomplished portrait of Leo. She confided to me that a secret message, for her eyes alone, was written in invisible ink at the bottom of the photograph. Nothing could have impressed me more unless it had been the revelation that Leo was a spy. Chrissie's looks had changed. The girlish fluffiness had been replaced by something much smoother and more languorous, which I put down to the battery of American cosmetics displayed around the bedroom and the new hairdressing techniques culled from Joanna. But there was something else. The atmosphere was charged with an emotion I recognized from all the films I had watched in the dark closeness of the Langham cinema. I also knew that only the young and the beautiful could experience such a feeling. This ruled out my parents, Chrissie's parents, most of the inhabitants of my known world and, certainly, knobbly-kneed eleven-year-olds.

I used to pray that Chrissie and Leo could live happily ever after and that Eddie and little Morris would evaporate. In fact, Leo got a posting to a far distant unit. Chrissie's parents were away visiting relatives the night Leo told her, and after he had gone she howled like a wolf. I was asleep in my small boxroom and the inhuman noises woke me up. I felt terrified until I identified the sounds and then I went downstairs to try to comfort her.

Sometimes I would walk round the authorized outer fringes of the Hall grounds looking for small flowers and savouring the rich smell of the surrounding greenery, murmuring to myself: 'A violet by a mossy stone, half-hidden from the eye', full of the romantic yearning that permeated the house, and which in my case centred on one Roy Redshaw, a boy in my class at the village school. He was acknowledged to be clever and marked out for the grammar school. I always felt terribly inferior to him because I thought my obsession with him must show whereas his feelings for me (if he had any) were masked by remarkable indifference. I think I perceived even then that although I was perhaps as intelligent as Roy, my potential would always be dissipated by such sentimental hankering. After hours of being a half-hidden violet I would go home and one look in the mirror would disperse all illusions. No one would ever love that nose.

My mother wrote to say that I had passed my scholarship to Thoresby High School, so I went back to the ruins. The streets looked liked mouths from which every alternate tooth had been inexpertly extracted. I joined the Baptist church, for the singing, and transferred my affections from Roy Redshaw to a small, fair-haired boy called Spud Spurgeon. He was much more encouraging and he reciprocated the note I passed him during prayers with one which read, 'Meet me at the back of the Nautical College at 4 o'clock.' I remembered, with great sadness, the chaste kiss we exchanged during that short tryst when, in 1974, I read his name in the local newspaper – Spud Spurgeon, Wireless Operator – on the crew list of the trawler, *Gaul,* which was lost with all hands in Arctic waters.

Three

I had immense freedom during my adolescence. My parents had had so little education themselves that they would not have known how to direct or interfere with mine. Lacking any pressure to do my homework thoroughly, I whipped through it in record time and was soon out roaming the streets with my friends. (The absence of the motor car made streets much more friendly places than they are now.) We dared each other to sneak into the side entrance of the flicks, chalked rude words on walls, or congregated outside the brightly-lit fish-and-chip shop or beer-off for long joke-telling sessions until bed-time. Inside the house there was no privacy, for all activities took place communally in the one heated room. Working in your bedroom was considered to be peculiar and it was freezing cold up there anyway. So I painted pictures, wrote poems and read stories to the accompaniment of the radio, Harry's chisel splinterings, Dad's hammer blows and Mum on the sewing-machine. If next door happened to be having a row, I would strain my ears to catch the additional entertainment. Such living may not have been ideal but it was always cosy. Too old for toys and too young for boys – those pre-teen years were so awkward unless you had well-heeled and strong-minded parents who booted you off to the Girl Guides, violin lessons and the tennis club.

From early childhood I greedily gobbled all the literature in the small branch library which was scarcely two doors away from my house, and I pestered the librarians for all sorts of esoteric items. 'Can I have *The Shahnameh* by Firdausi, please? You don't seem to have it on the shelves.' Miss Senior, my English teacher, had lent me Matthew Arnold's *Collected Poems* and I had been so stirred by *Sohrab* and *Rustum* that I wanted to read the Persian source work. Another time, hunting for classics, I pounced on Rabelais's *Gargantua and Pantagruel* and gleefully pulled it from the shelf only to find that it was a block of wood. On its side was written, 'You must ask the librarian for this book.' I did and was told that it was not suitable for a child: 'Come back in four years' time.' My reading was wide but whimsical. When I went to Hull University, over twenty years later, I was able to fill in the gaps. My parents had no books of their own, apart from the Bible, and a dingy history series bought at the door from a travelling salesman. Before her marriage, when my mother was in service, the cultured Unitarian family she worked for gave her the run of their bookshelves. Although she was still an avid reader, she could not afford to buy books, nor could she see the point in buying them when the public library was so close by. She was a keen reader of novels and biographies but she did not share my love of poetry – in fact until adolescence, I met no one who did.

While still at school I joined two jazz clubs and supplemented these twice-weekly fixes with furtive sessions listening to AFN (the American Forces Network) on the wireless after my parents had gone to bed. They were solid music-hall fans and had no time for either 'agony music' (classical) or 'that blasted racket' (jazz and swing).

Mum, Dad and I enjoyed going to the pictures together and did so regularly. Spencer Tracy films were our favourites. We always went at 6.30 p.m regardless of when the programme started. I got so used to arriving in the middle of a film, deducing what had happened so far, then seeing it round to the point at which we had come in, that I felt robbed of a necessary guessing-game when I first began watching films from beginning to end.

School was definitely at the bottom of my list of interests. When I was fourteen I had to choose one of the three vocational courses offered. Thoresby was classed as a central school (a sort of technical grammar school) and at that time pupils could not take a School Certificate to qualify them for higher education, though I think it was introduced not long after I left. The three courses to choose from were the pre-nursing, the practical (you bathed dolls, scrubbed floors and washed clothes in preparation for a job as a domestic servant) and the commercial, for which I opted. So, for a few hours a week, the usual school curriculum was varied with Pitman's shorthand, double-entry accounts and keyboard practice. It was a two-year course but I left it after one year when I was fifteen and only half-trained. My parents were happy for me to leave school since, for them, the main goal in life was to get out to work to earn some money. In any case, I had untruthfully assured them that I was a whizzo typist who did not need another year's training.

I must have been insufferable in my early teens. I found it easy to patronize the family with my highfalutin notions and highbrow reading matter. 'What's that you're reading, Jean?' 'It's T. S. Eliot's *The Waste Land,* but you wouldn't understand it.' If the truth be told, I didn't understand it either but the sound of it was marvellous. Or I would be draped across the leatherette couch, my face covered in a mudpack and a slice of cucumber clapped over each eyelid, following the latest hint *Woman's Own* had recommended for acne and tired eyes. 'When are you going to wash these pots, Jean?' Mother would ask. 'When I've finished this.' *This* might be the painstaking embroidering of *Ted Heath Fan Club* (the band leader, of course, not the politician) on the reverse of my old navy blue, vee-necked, school pullover, now worn back to front to disguise its origin. On other nights I would have endless giggling and whispering orgies with my friend Audrey from next door.

My parents were patient, tolerant and encouraged me to bring home my boy-friends, although mother wished that more of them had proper jobs and was baffled when they introduced themselves as writers or poets. They mostly worked in shops or offices but could not bring themselves to admit it. After they had eaten supper with us and gone off into the night, my mother would say to me, 'I wish you'd find a nice boiler-maker. You can't beat a lad with a trade.' Her world picture was somewhat medieval in that she had strong notions of hierarchy and where we all fitted into it. 'Know your place' was one of her oft-repeated sayings. I have no doubt that she was taught this at school and in domestic service, but I am sure it was a view shared by the majority of her class. It did not do to try and get above yourself. She and my father had achieved their highest ambition for each other: he was proud that he could afford for her not to go out to work after their marriage; she was content that he had a steady job, that they could pay their way and have a week's annual holiday at the seaside.

My first job was as a junior shorthand typist with a small firm of accountants who paid me a pound a week. Fifteen shillings went to Mum for my keep and I had five bob pocket-money which was supposed to cover my entertainment, bus fares and clothes, though Mum still made me the odd dress or skirt. I blew my first week's pocket-money on a book of poems by Edith Sitwell, which did not stand the test of time. I was more selective thereafter.

The job was not terribly demanding and offered a fair bit of variety. First thing in the morning I took a small jug to Charlie's, a bakery in the old part of town. He also sold milk. After queuing up with the other office juniors and the town's tramps to whom Charlie dispensed, free of charge, yesterday's stale buns, I took my two-pennyworth of milk back to the office and picked up the local post for hand delivery to nearby banks, solicitors and the Inspector of Taxes. I then presented myself to the partners, ready and eager to take dictation. Mr Greenfield, the younger partner, winced when he saw he had drawn me instead of Jean, the older and more competent typist. My imperfect grasp of accountancy jargon meant that he would have to dictate at snail-slow pace for the next hour. He did not like my tea-making either. I had discovered that if I put the minimum amount of tea in the pot, over three weeks I could fiddle sixpence out of the petty cash. Mr Greenfield would plead with Jean, 'Can't you teach Joan how to make a decent pot of tea?' My name had been changed to Joan to avoid confusion over two Jeans. They announced the change to me on my first day and I was annoyed that they had not chosen something more suitable, such as Christabel or Madeleine.

During my year there Jean knocked my typing into shape and taught me the rudiments of office practice. I was going through a period of rebellion against everything home-made and so, daily, Jean and I swapped our packing up. I ate her neat, white-sliced-bread-with-Silver-Shred-marmalade sandwiches, and gave her my home-baked bread, cheddar-cheese-filled doorstoppers. I was happy there. The audit clerks who buzzed in for a few weeks at a time were a lively lot and one of them was a music lover. 'Listen to Tchaikovsky's *Caprice Espagnol*. It's like . . . your first pint of beer. Oh, and there's Ravel's *Bolero* on the Third – that's as good as making love,' he said on his way out to do the egg-and-bacon merchant's audit. I could not appreciate the comparisons but I straightaway combed through the *Radio Times* to find the pieces and put rings round them. My first job of the week was marking the programmes that must be listened to at all costs.

What really irked me all the time I worked in offices was the humiliating business of asking for a rise. I would sweat over the thought of it for days, knowing the deed had to be done and agonizing over the correct form of words. The smile on the boss's face would fade to gloom as soon as the five-letter word 'money' was mentioned and then the bartering would begin. God would ask, 'How much were you thinking of?' 'Well, could you manage five shillings, please?' His saintly old hand would pass over his suffering brow. 'We've had a bad year, an awfully bad year and overheads are up. I'm afraid we can only go to half a crown.' His sad, accompanying smile indicated both triumph and the end of the interview. My sick feeling of relief at having the ordeal over would be tempered by disappointment. But habits of deference were too deeply ingrained in me to see the discrepancy between the offer the stingy old sod had made me and the fact that he had just bought himself a new motor car or a mansion in the country. (Years later, when I started teaching, I thanked providence for the trade union, the equal pay, the pension rights and the salary scale.) Comparing notes with other juniors in the queue at Charlie's convinced me that I should look for a better paid job.

Throughout my childhood and early adolescence I had a talent for catching lice, scabies, fleas, impetigo, worms and all the other nasties that my mother claimed only dirty people got. She thought that perhaps, in my case, such susceptibility to anti-social complaints stemmed from having always been a sickly and ailing child and that, therefore, it was her duty to 'build-me-up'. She was part of the pre-National Health generation that worried constantly about running up doctors bills that they would not be able to pay. Preventive medicine came cheaper than doctors: one bad illness could incur debts that would beggar the family for years.

To strengthen me, my mother dosed me with every patent remedy on the chemist's shelves; not to mention the alternative potions that she bought from dispensaries and herbalists. Scott's Emulsion, brimstone and treacle, Pink Pills, senna tea, lincti of every shade, worming tablets, cod-liver oil and malt – all were regularly thrust down me. I was also encouraged to eat daily a bowl of milky pap called Benger's Food, a sort of thin gritty porridge that made me feel sick. Even when I was sixteen, and in my second job, working as a secretary to the manager of the most unfashionable and shabby department store in Hull, mother would make sure I took my jollop.

Willis's sold pretty dull stuff, perhaps some of the clothes were good but on two pounds ten shillings a week I couldn't afford any of them, and I was not interested in shops anyway except for bookshops and the beauty counter at the chemists. The offices were old and squalid, with rude wooden benches and clapped-out typewriters that regularly jumped half a line in the middle of a letter. Rat-traps were discreetly tucked away in corners. The store itself had money tubes that zinged along wires and came shooting up into the cashier's slot of a room that was tacked on to the general office. I was once asked to take a message to the 'Mantle Department' and looked all over the store for fireplaces or gas-brackets before I discovered that it was the coat department.

All the employees paid in sixpence a week for the firm's annual day trip to Bridlington. One Thursday (half-day closing) before the July sales, after having posed for a group photo lined up in front of the charabanc, we took off. Faces that normally looked as though they had just taken a sniff from a vinegar bottle, were relaxed and even Mr Craft, the perennially worried-looking manager, was in smiling holiday mood. It was my first experience of a firm's outing and I had no idea that the whole purpose of the expedition was to pile in and out of as many licensed premises as possible. At each country pub, the locals would hutch up into corners to make room for our large party. My friend Pam, the accounts and invoice typist, would muscle her way to the piano and vamp out rousing versions of 'Daisy, Daisy, Give me your answer do' and 'When Irish eyes are smiling'. I sat, prim and embarrassed in my office suit and cream corduroy bucket-shaped hat, trying to feel part of the crowd and gingerly sipping the sour-tasting beer the cashier had bought me. Snob that I was, I could not reconcile myself to the fact that I had sacrificed my usual visit to the Continental Cinema and thereby missed a Gerard Philippe film. Art came before life in my book. Fun was being had, though: the Lingerie Buyer flirted decorously with the Brylcreemed whippet from Floor Coverings, and even the faces of the enamelled and golden-haired ladies from Cosmetics and Hosiery cracked the occasional smile as the evening wore on. The fish and chips, the fortune teller on Bridlington's prom., the unaccustomed beer and the jolting of the bus eventually took their toll and halfway through the journey back, my face turned as green as my suit. The coach driver, having stopped twice for me to dodge behind a hedge, would brook no further delays for it was now quite late, everyone was keen to get home and I was spoiling the general jollity. As we sped along the dark country lanes, I sat on the coach steps vomiting copiously into my corduroy hat. The manager came up and patted my shoulder every so often and said, 'There, there, Miss Holland' through a background of 'Roll out the Barrel'. When I got home and staggered through the door, head buzzing and muscles aching from the internal revolution, I found a note from my mum which read, 'Your Benger's Food is in the oven.'

The two most formative influences during my teenage years were my cousin Joyce and the Workers' Educational Association, to which she introduced me. My father had two older brothers, Oscar and Alf, of whom we saw very little although they too lived in Hull. When they left school, my paternal grandfather – a ship's engineer – took them to sea to work as trimmers on steam-powered trawlers. They eventually qualified as Chief Engineers. At the outbreak of the First World War, Alf and Oscar joined the Royal Navy and worked on minesweepers stationed at Gibraltar. They left the sea at the end of the hostilities and were determined to better themselves. Alf bought a motorbike, fitted it with a wooden box, a marble slab, some portable scales and started a peripatetic wet-fish business. Eventually, he was able to buy his own premises and set up shop. Oscar began his trading with a pushbike, a suitcaseful of elastic, tape, pins, other haberdashery items and a pedlar's licence. He graduated from the pushbike to a motor-bike and sidecar, which was also an ideal conveyance for the family. When I knew him, he was a Labour councillor, he worked as a commercial traveller and he owned his own car.

Oscar was the eldest brother and a great one for self-improvement; he had attended WEA psychology classes before the Second World War. His eldest daughter, Maidie, was a bit of a stay-at-home, so he encouraged her to join the Association in the hope that it would broaden her life. The official age for joining was eighteen but Maidie's young sister, Joyce, who had just left school, was keen to be involved and so she went along too. Joyce, a real live-wire and a splendid organizer, encouraged her other like-minded young friends to join and they were allowed to form a youth section. This meant they could attend the socials, the very popular Saturday night Topical Talks and even the classes, although their names were probably not put on the register.

The membership consisted of a mixed bag of workers and intellectuals who, naturally, did not always see eye to eye. The workers felt that the spirit of the WEA would be lost if the intellectuals were allowed to dominate it. Frank Nicholson, a gentle, highly-cultured, ex-Beverley Grammar School teacher was the tutor-organizer. He led from behind and kept the whole boiling in equilibrium. In the early 1940s a large house on Spring Bank was acquired as a headquarters. Frank Nicholson, or Nick as he was affectionately called, had rooms on the top floor and, during lectures or Topical Talks, the tantalizing smell of Nick's dinner would waft down to the listeners. Much interest was taken in the decoration of the rooms to be used for classes and there was controversy over the colour scheme for the lecture room. Rita Bronowsky decreed that one wall should be painted red since red was said to be the colour to stimulate thought. Old Mr Dorsey and others thought this was awful and used all the leftover ends of paint mixed together to make a sort of sludge, with which they covered it. Some fine beech-wood chairs were purchased from the Peace Pledge Union, which had bought them from Finland before the war.

Having a headquarters and lots of social activities meant that people from all the different classes, which had previously been held in a number of different venues, could now meet together. The socials were very good and helped raise money for the premises. These evenings began with party games such as 'spin the plate' and progressed to ballroom dancing and a raffle. Then the refreshments were served. They consisted of lemonade, cakes and very small sandwiches for, although the war was over, food was still in short supply. Such entertainments may seem quaint by today's more sophisticated standards but ours was a naïve generation and we found the socials delightful. They also had distinct advantages over the discos I sometimes go to nowadays: since there were limits to the volume the wind-up gramophone could achieve, we were able to hold conversations and dance at the same time. The proximity was nice too.

There was always something going on and the activities ranged from Sunday night play-readings to weekend hikes and cycle rides. Music recitals were given on Nick's gramophone, there was a wide selection of books to borrow and there one could read unaffordable magazines such as the *New Statesman* and *The Times Literary Supplement*. Here, under one roof, was a wealth of intellectual nourishment that one might never otherwise have come across.

I particularly enjoyed the Sunday night play-readings when Nick would borrow from the public library a set of plays by Synge, Shaw, Ibsen or O'Casey and a group of us would endeavour to delight the audience with our reading. Being the youngest female, and a show-off, I was often asked to read the ingenue parts and I could not wait to get my teeth into Deirdre of the Sorrows or the Maid of Orleans. Afterwards, Nick gravely complimented us on our performances as the tea and biscuits went the rounds and the social part of the evening got into full swing. When I was young, the Hull WEA was the very best club you could join.

There was always a wide selection of lectures on offer and I attended many, on a variety of subjects. When Richard Hoggart began his Adult Education Extension literature classes, I joined up, and this became the high point of my week. Miss Senior at Thoresby High School encouraged my bookishness, but there was a limit to the attention she could give to one pupil in a class of forty-odd. For the first time my reading was given some direction and, since Richard always encouraged us to do homework (which he marked with great thoroughness), I also received criticism. He did me a great service by blue-pencilling the more maudlin portions of my dreadful poems.

We working-class would-be intellectuals were very earnest and therefore easily snubbed. I remember telling a snooty boy-friend, destined for Oxford, that I had been reading Lorca and Yeats (which I pronounced Yeets since that was how you pronounced Keats). He could not comment on Lorca since he had not read him but his crushingly condescending 'Oh, you mean Yates' made me blush with shame. Nor had I any idea that Oxford comprised a set of colleges rather than just one, until a less snooty boy-friend, who was taking me home one night, shouted down the path: 'Please write to me.' 'Where shall I write?' I asked. 'Jesus, Cambridge', he answered and I thought he was being blasphemous until he explained the collegiate system to me.

I found a matching earnestness in Richard Hoggart, an

inspiring teacher, who took us all seriously and tried very hard to correct our often sloppy and subjective thinking. He was marvellous at deflecting potty questions or gently steering us back to George Herbert or John Donne when some old lady had drifted into a digression about how well her chrysanthemums were doing. At fifteen, I was by far the youngest in his group and he would come up to me sometimes at the end of a session and say, wistfully, 'Miss Holland, don't you know any factory girls who would like to join the class?' He was keen to share his cultural world with the less lucky and to raise people's expectations of themselves – an example I have tried to follow in my work at the Hull College of Further Education. It also pleased me that, when George Hartley and I began our publishing venture, Richard was usually the first to send his cheque and order for whatever our subscription form offered.

My cousin Joyce stopped being an active participator in WEA activities in 1948, a year after I joined, for she married Steve Ramsey, a widower, who had a five-year-old son, Paul. Her time was taken up with a full-time teaching job and meeting the needs of her family but she and Steve generously took me under their wing, provided me with another cultural lifeline and allowed me to feel that theirs was my second home.

To reach the Ramseys, one took a longish bus journey to Stoneferry, a heavily industrialized area on the east of the River Hull. The bus wound its way round the river, passing flea-pit cinemas, evil-smelling oil and cake mills, fish and pig manure processors and soap and cement factories, until it reached an enclave of prefabs, one of which was theirs. Joyce and Steve made me so welcome that my visits soon became institutionalized. Every Tuesday, bearing a loaf of bread baked by my mother, I went straight from work, spent the evening there and stayed the night.

To me, their house was a miracle of modern design – snug and functional. (These temporary dwellings, which were intended to last for only ten years, are still a part of

Hull's housing stock; up to a few years ago, Hull had the largest proportion of the country's prefabs.) I deemed it the greatest of sybaritic pleasures to take a bath in porcelain instead of zinc, use an indoor loo that had a handle instead of a chain, and wash dishes in a fitted kitchen that boasted a draining-board, lots of cupboards and a fridge. But it was the decor that really impressed me. At home we had patterned wallpaper, brown paintwork (because it didn't show the dirt), offcuts of flowered carpet and an assortment of dowdy framed prints purchased in 1923 (when Mum and Dad married) with titles such as *Honeymoon in Venice* and *Highland Cattle*. Joyce's walls were painted matt white; there were shelves which displayed choice pieces of pottery; a haunting Paul Nash print dominated one wall; the fitted carpet was plain and there were rows of books on a wide variety of subjects.

Steve, a large man and older than Joyce, alarmed me at first. I knew that he did a quite ordinary job, working as a goods checker on the railway, and yet his knowledge was encyclopaedic. As a private soldier in the REME during the war, he had taught himself a number of foreign languages. The first time I really met him, which was some time after his and Joyce's wedding, he was typing out a story he had translated from the Swedish. I soon realized that Steve's slightly aloof manner was the result of shyness and that he was by nature a man who liked to observe rather than hold the centre of the stage. As I grew up, I came to appreciate keenly his dry wit and generous heart.

Joyce was for me the 'compleat woman'. Even in her early twenties she had that enviable combination of intellect and practicality that I have tried to copy and always just missed: my logic does not bear scrutiny and my pastry is as heavy as lead. Good at everything she attempted, Joyce was particularly keen to cut a dash with her cooking but Steve and Paul were disappointingly conservative when it came to food. I always appreciated novelty, so she saved her experiments up for Tuesday nights. I would bound in with, 'That smells good, Joyce. What is it?' 'Mackerel in gooseberry sauce', she answered, 'followed by Mushrooms in a Meadow.' She placed the dessert on the table with a flourish, and revealed a grouping of dome-shaped meringues with chocolate frilled undersides and banana stalks set in a bed of green jelly. It seemed very adventurous stuff in those pre-Elizabeth David days. My mother was a brilliant cook of plain, traditional English dishes but, although I knew how lucky I was, I hankered after more exotic cuisine. After a lifetime of dishing up three square meals a day, Mum now worked to a formula. One could accurately predict that there would be soup and hash on Monday, liver and onions on Tuesday, steak on Wednesday, sausages on Thursday and fish on Friday. After a decade, one or two items might be changed and other fixtures substituted.

Sometimes there would be just Joyce, Steve, Paul and me but often there were visitors, some of whom are still my friends. Frank Redpath (who was in his Gulley Jimson phase at the time) was a regular caller, Fred Singleton (who was always on his way to or from Finland or Yugoslavia), and many others. They were all a few years older than I was and most of them were busily following up interests in politics, art, languages, history or literature. The Ramseys' door was ever open and, although they did not have much money, their friends were always welcome to eat, drink, discourse and be merry. The evenings I spent there showed me a stylish, more liberal kind of existence and made me realize that you could live the intellectual life in Hull as easily as London.

Four

At sixteen I decided to diversify my musical and literary activities with Good Works so, with my friend Audrey, I joined a predominantly Quaker organization, the International Voluntary Service for Peace. We cleaned and decorated the houses of old age pensioners, knitted bootees and painted cots at the Home for Unmarried Mothers at Sutton, and in my two week summer holiday from Willis's (Audrey was at a grammar school) we travelled to Leeds to make a children's playing field out of what appeared to be a small mountain. Every morning an international gang would leave the hostel with spades and pickaxes to worry away at huge chunks of rock. At the end of each day we filed into the municipal baths and washed away the grime (Oh, the bliss of lying in a deep tubful of hot water, calling for 'more hot in number seven, please'), and sang French, German and English folk-songs as we walked through the streets back to the hostel for our evening meal. Afterwards we carried on with 'The Foggy Foggy Dew' and 'Chevaliers de la Table Ronde' until sleep overtook us. Not being very adept with pickaxes, we arrived back in Hull looking rather scabby but feeling immensely well-travelled and determined to go further afield the following year. There was a farming scheme in Poitiers; we signed up for that since we were now far too sophisticated to share family hols with my parents in the caravan they usually rented in Withernsea.

I expect most adults are tortured by the shame they now

feel about their adolescent snobberies. My parents were such a good, self-sacrificing pair, scratting and scraping all the year round so that I could enjoy for a week what they had never had even for a day in their own childhoods. As kids, the furthest they had ever got from the warren of closely packed houses of the Hessle Road fishing community was to Little Switzerland, a sprawling, abandoned chalk quarry four miles away, scrounging a lift there on a coal cart and walking back, carrying in jamjars the tiddlers they had caught.

To be part of the peasantry in Poitiers was a pleasing prospect for the summer of 1951 – meantime, it was back to my usual social round. One night at the WEA I met Peter, although he was not a regular attender. Peter was widely read and he wrote poetry non-stop. Maybe paper was in short supply in his house – most things were – for his handwriting was as microscopic as Emily Dickinson's. He was a slim, dark-haired, hungry-looking youth with a long, strongly-modelled face, a soft, well-modulated voice and an intense manner. His facial expressions were a map of his shifting moods, expressing Byronic scorn at one moment and excitement about some new person or literary find, the next.

During the short time we knew each other, he sent me a poem or a letter every day – invariably addressed to 'Dearest Antigone', for everyone he knew became part of his private mythology. He felt, more strongly than any of my contemporaries, the need to escape from the constraints of his narrow home and he was impatient to shrug off the provinciality of Hull. We were all steeped in a culture purveyed by the middle-class writers we read and whose characters we strove to emulate. It was a way of coping with the greyness of post-war reality. One might appear to be selling socks in a shabby gents' outfitters or typing an advertisement for ladies' outsize vests but in the mind one was playing out a part in an Aldous Huxley novel or Jean Anouilh drama. Apart from D. H. Lawrence's early characters, there were no romantic literary role-models close to our own situation to identify with and so we chose to be Isherwood's Sally Bowles, Fitzgerald's Gatsby or Hemingway's Lady Brett. When Peter met me, I think I had taken a dive backwards to the Middle Ages and was playing Helen Waddell's Heloise . . . It must all have been very painful for our parents.

Peter and I were dazzled by each other for at least a fortnight, during which time I twice went home with him, ostensibly to look at his Journals. Their humble house backed on to an open drain on the east side of town. His father was dead and his mother had worked hard to bring up her three children decently, but the home was threadbare and I could see why Peter needed to transfer his friends and family from their drab surroundings to the bright, legendary world of his imagination. After tea and the Journals came the seduction. I wrangled feebly and mentioned the danger of babies. He countered energetically with some plausible-sounding stuff about D.H. Lawrence and the phases of the moon. Who was I to argue with a man who was not only a fount of esoteric knowledge but had also done it before? Two weeks later we had a blazing row. I had annoyed him by making a disdainful comment on a book we had both read. He called me a supercilious cow (it did not take long for our breeding to show) and, always quick to fire when given the right spark, I shrieked back at him. The last words shouted from one side of the Boulevard to the other by one or both of us were, 'Don't think I want to see *you* any more.' I mooned about for a day or two, as you do at that age, vacillating between anger and misery, and then I forgot him. That was definitely the end of that. Or so we thought.

A month or so later, I began to feel peculiar. Science at school had seemed to consist of learning the names of the private parts of a flower, or doing something incomprehensible with a bunsen burner, so I was thunderstruck when my doctor told me I was pregnant. I could say farewell to Poitiers, or anywhere else for that matter. Callous and self-centred, as only a frightened seventeen-year-old can be, I had no intention of bringing up a baby; I certainly did not want to be married and rejected the gallant but half-hearted offer Peter made when he learned of my state. The only way out, I thought, was to present myself to Matron at the aforementioned home for unmarried mothers, have the baby there and then offer it up for adoption. Matron was shocked to see me at the door on a non-cot-painting night and her surprised response to my tale was, 'Not a *nice* girl like you, Jean!'

Two months later when I broke the news to my parents, they were similarly devastated, but hurt too. At the time I was angry at what I interpreted as their puritanism, and there was an element of that, but I can see now how disappointed they must have been for me and for themselves. Having grown up in homes macerated by deprivation, they had both slaved to rise above their early lives to a level of working-class respectability where nourishing meals appeared regularly and there was a set of clothes for Sunday as well as those for every day. They could not afford to let Harry, who was very bright, take up the scholarship he won to the grammar school but they did the next best thing and helped him to get a good apprenticeship, and they were proud to see me avoid Smith and Nephews factory and get less well paid but higher status jobs in offices. What was there for me now but the prospect of sinking into the soft underbelly of Hessle Road sloth, becoming one of the brigade of prematurely aged young women – with no husband, no teeth, no figure and no self-respect. After they had calmed down a bit, they conceded that I should not marry Peter if I did not love him, and they readily fell in with my plan to take sanctuary at Sutton House and tell the relations and friends that I had gone to Poitiers. (Audrey bravely went on her own and, at discreet intervals, obligingly posted sets of postcards that I had pre-written.)

At one point during the dreadful weeks at home before I

44

departed for Sutton House, my father said to me, sadly, 'Why didn't you remember your rubber goods?' Since this was the first time anything of the kind had been mentioned, I shrugged the question off, too embarrassed at this late stage to admit that I didn't know about them. Of course I had been seeing them all my life. You could not live down Hessle Road without tripping over them down every back alley, but that did not mean that I understood their use or how easy it was to conceive.

As an infant I heard more about not sex itself, but its effects, than I ever did later on, when it might have made some difference to my actions. Drinking cups of sweet tea in the houses of my mother's friends, I would hear gruesome snippets such as, 'She nearly died with Wilf; she was sat over a bucket of blood for three hours', or 'Bella was fifty-four when she got caught with their Enid; caught on change, you know, and *he* never looked after her . . .' Then seeing my interest, they would say 'Little pitchers have big ears', purse their lips and change the subject. Once I found in Mum's bottom drawer an antique pamphlet which contained one or two anatomical drawings and an engraving of something that resembled a rubber pudding-basin. My cousin Joyce, during a similar rummaging sessions, unearthed a tin of French chalk and some little balloons. We were none the wiser.

As I grew older, the occasional veiled reference was made. My mother would warn me, after I had stayed out half an hour later than my bedtime, 'If you get into trouble, it'll be the doorstep for you.' I was pretty sure what trouble was, but not very clear about how you got into it. Even menstruation was passed over without any explanation of its significance. Mum simply presented me with a home-made drawstring bag full of oblong pads. They were fashioned from many layers of old flannelette sheeting piled on top of each other and neatly stitched round the edges. 'Change them regularly and put them out for boiling when you've finished' was the total sum of the information I was given at this watershed in my life. Four years later, at the age of fifteen, I decided that – hang the expense – I would rather bung up the S bend with Dr White's than be the only girl in Hull who wore tailor-made S.T.'s.

My mother often said, without elaboration, that I was a mistake. After my parents were both dead, Aunt Madge told me that my mother was pregnant with Harry when she married my father. Two mistakes. But to have slipped up only twice in forty years of married life argues either an adroitness with contraceptive techniques or an absence of sex. They behaved so lovingly towards each other that I do not think the latter can have been the case. When he was in a good mood, and he usually was, Dad would come in from work, pick my mother up in his arms and dance round the room with her. She and I delighted in his great smacking kisses and bear hugs.

One can see the difficulties of living at such close quarters. The way working-class couples dealt with the semi-public nature of sex in small, crowded houses was simply not to mention it. How else could dignity and decorum be maintained? There were so few occasions when couples could be alone together that this side of their private lives was pushed into a very small corner. The trouble was, of course, that by pretending sex did not exist, and by failing to pass on their hard-won knowledge, girls such as myself grew up to be just as ignorant and un-prepared as their mothers had been.

It was implicit that the ever-interesting topic was one you learned about after you were married, not before. Any prior knowledge indicated a leaning towards promiscuity. Ask a group of women of my age why they got married and half of them will answer, 'Because I had to.'

The other great barrier against enlightenment is one that remains unaffected by time and social class: parents find it difficult to come to terms with their own children's, espe-cially their daughters', sexuality. They decide that the

46

strong feelings they felt as youngsters were an aberration. They hope that if they pretend sexual awakening is not there, it might just go away. Time and time again, women have smugly told me that their nubile young daughters are 'not interested in boys' and I have wondered who they thought they were kidding.

Five

Matron, a strict but good-hearted Anglican maiden lady in her seventies, ran Sutton House on behalf of the Moral Welfare division of the church with the help of her side-kick, a nervy woman who, after her children had grown up, tried unsuccessfully to become a nun. There was also Nurse who came in daily to help with the babies. She was a humane, down-to-earth Nottinghamshire woman who had known D. H. Lawrence at Greasley Board School. She would not enlarge on this acquaintanceship further than to remark professionally, 'Bert always had a snotty nose'. The work of the house was done by the inmates, whose average residence was five months – three months before the birth and two months after – and, since Sylvia and I were a cut above, we were given the privileged position of personal servants to Matron and her senile dog, William. Sylvia, a twenty-four-year-old schoolteacher, was admitted shortly after I was, and she saved me from going insane.

Every day we cleaned Matron's bedroom, bathroom and sitting-room, Cardinal-polished the corridor, filled the coal scuttles, made her bed turning the counterpane corner back just so, fed beastly William, sliced wafer-thin bread (my job – Sylvia could only manage wodges) and served at the staff table. One important day when a deaconess had come to stay and I could scarcely balance a tray in front of my protuberance, I dropped a soft-boiled egg on the coconut matting. The failed nun tut-tutted and matron's martyred voice reached me as I scrubbed at the mess with my hanky: *I'll* do without, Jean.'

The rules and prohibitions were endless: we must not divulge our surnames to each other (sensible, I suppose), or discuss our lives or how we came to be in this situation (the myth being that we had all conceived immaculately); we could not use a telephone, nor go out of the house except in a crocodile headed by the would-be nun and we could only have one visitor (female) for one hour every three weeks. Smoking was absolutely forbidden but, on receiving an urgent SOS from me, either Audrey or Peter tried to smuggle ten Woodbines in to me by removing the bottom layer of a box of Black Magic and substituting the cigarettes. Matron, wise to the tricks of old lags, intercepted them and gave me a most fearful lecture.

As a treat, we had hymn singing two nights a week and on Sundays we attended three religious ceremonies, two in Sutton House chapel and then we crocodiled down to Sutton church for the other one. There the girls from the local mental asylum, who sat in pews in front of us, turned round, giggled and pointed their fingers at our bellies because, although they were not all there, they were not so daft that they did not know what was wrong with us.

Two by two we walked back past the stunted hawthorn hedges and the riding-school, nipping smartly out of the way of the arrogant young equestrians in their caps and jodhurs, who so reminded the would-be nun of her Jocelyn and Adrian when they were young. She talked loudly about the lovely home she had given up to come and minister to us, while Sylvia and I straggled behind trying to discuss life, death, poetry and the differences in our backgrounds.

Pagan to the core, I learned a grudging respect for Sylvia's contemplative brand of religion. To me Christianity represented at worst an injunction to feel guilt, at best a chance to bellow hymns, so I was astonished to hear her confident and cultured voice asking Matron, 'Where is the chapel? How often does the priest come? Can I have a locker for my books?' My heart warmed at the prospect of a supplement to my small hoard of books. Every few weeks Sylvia received from a friend a parcel containing volumes of Simone Weil, Simone de Beauvoir, Kirkgaard, Andrew Lang, etc. She was also unique in being the only one of us who wanted to have and keep a baby. Every afternoon, during our two hours of free time, she went to the chapel for private prayer and meditation. When did she read the books? Perhaps when I was strip-washing. I had developed a neurotic compulsion to wash all over about seven times a day. Malodorous Morag seemed to have the opposite compulsion. She shared with me one of the only two centrally-heated rooms and I could never decide whether it was me or Morag who smelled worst. 'Do I smell?' I anxiously asked Sylvia. 'Yes, you silly. It's all that Coty *L'aimant* soap.'

There were no medical facilities at Sutton House so when labour started, you were taken by ambulance to Hedon Road Maternity Hospital for ten days to give birth and recover. Matron kindly advised us to buy Woolworth wedding rings and said that the nurses had been primed to call us Mrs to avoid the ignominy and to shield us from the barbs of our decently wed bedfellows.

Many of my friends faded away during that period of my life and almost everyone who knew about my fall from grace made me feel that I was tainted goods: 'Will any mercer take another's ware/When once tis tous'd and sullied?' A few hours after Laurien was born, the pretty young woman in the next bed made a conversational opening to me with, 'I had six bridesmaids at my wedding. How many did you have? 'Eight', I replied, miserably, and turned my face to the wall.

Sylvia's daughter was born early on Christmas Day 1951. The press photographer had weaselled his way in, intent on producing a big sentimental splash for the front page of the *Hull Daily Mail*. Pleased as punch, he clicked away then asked Sylvia for her name. 'Miss Sylvia Cress-well', she answered. 'You mean missis.' 'No, I don't. I mean Miss.' 'Can I put missis?' 'You most certainly cannot.' Sylvia was far too highly principled to have truck with any kind of subterfuge. So he retired, disappointed and embarrassed by her frankness, to wait for a legitimate baby to hatch.

The moment Laurien was born, everything else became insignificant. The unintended lump, that I had tried so hard for nine months to dissociate myself from, had two shell-pink ears, a lovely big light-bulb-shaped forehead and perfect, clutching little fingers. How could I have ever thought I would want to disown a person I was so completely responsible for? How could I give her away to a stranger who might turn out to be a prude, a hypocrite or a psychotic child-bungler? If anyone were to make a mess of her upbringing, it would be me, though I would do my best to make life good for her. For a start, out went Petronella, her father's choice of name which, even with my limited experience, I could see would be her first handicap in the back streets of Hessle Road. At the time I did not realize how selfish I was in wanting to keep her. Nor was I prepared to face the fact that almost anyone could have offered her a higher material standard and a better start to life than I could. I excitedly told Matron, my first visitor, what I wanted to do, and after trying to dissuade me, she gave me all the practical help she could. (Two months later she found me a job as a live-in housekeeper to a family in Sutton. I did this work for six or more months until my parents invited me and Laurien back home.) What was so strange to me was my new-found feeling of protectiveness. I had never noticed babies or liked dolls. All I did with the latter was prop them up straight and wonder what other children found to do with them, when they could be outside playing Block or inside reading and painting.

Back at Sutton House the routines as a mother were different and harder. There was the same round of cleaning and washing but added to that was the breast-feeding and baby bathing. We were a mixed bunch. Not all of us had been blandished by a young man who cited the moon and D. H. Lawrence. (Oh, David Herbert! What a lot of mis-begetting you encouraged.) There were hairdressers misled by amorous married commercial travellers; a middle-aged housekeeper seduced then discarded by her employer; a half-Egyptian girl who worked in her father's café and did a sideshow at Hull Fair; a number of country girls who had fallen prey to hedge-bottom philanderers and a cool, dark-haired beauty who sanded and polished Queen Anne chair-legs for a living. The most tragic were the fourteen-year-old incest victims.

None of us were the hardened scarlet women we were often made to feel. Lily, the eel-catcher's daughter, had been beguiled by a US airman who promised her love and marriage until he found out she was pregnant; then photo-graphs of a previously undeclared wife and two kids in Wisconsin magically appeared on his dresser. Lily and I would stand together in the Dickensian laundry room, scrubbing stains out of nappies in sinks full of cold water. She held up the standard soap issue – a two-inch, evil-smelling square – and said, 'I bet this is people soap.' 'What's people soap, Lily?' 'It's what they made in Belsen out of rendered-down Jews. I reckon she bought a ship-load of it on the cheap.' Thinking about it now, there was probably very little money in the kitty to run the big house and feed us all, even with the help of our Maternity Grants.

The very worst times were when a baby was taken away for adoption. The adoptive parents came to the house and the girl would put a brave face on it until lights-out at 10.30. Then the crying started; great rending howls of anguish rang through the house all night as the bereft one refused to be pacified and each of us, even those who were keeping their babies, shared the grief.

Six

I had first met George Hartley four years earlier at the
Wheeler Street Youth Club in Hull, where one classroom
was devoted to a Rhythm Club. The year was 1947 and we
were both fourteen. About ten of us would gather there
one night a week to listen to recordings by bands such as
Tommy Dorsey, Benny Goodman, Woody Herman and
Stan Kenton. What we heard was limited to what Jim
owned, since Jim was the only one who had a gramophone
or any records. Jim, a beanpole youth with a slick of black
hair, was a few years older than most of us – he would be
about nineteen and no one was allowed to touch his
records or equipment. If you were Jim's girl-friend you
had made it. He would reverently place my favourite
record – Woody Herman's *Bijou* – on the turntable, crank
the handle, lift over the heavy arm, and off we would go,
each person miming a different instrument. I always
played the Bill Harris solo trombone bits, Jim would drum
on a desk, but George, who was formal and dignified,
merely tapped his foot. At some point word might go
round that Eddie had got five Woodbines so if you were
sharp you tried to sit next to him. When there was a lull, I
would go over to dark and brooding George who always
sat apart from the rest. He seemed shy but his confident,
well-spoken voice and his strong views contradicted that.
We would show one another the short stories and poems
we had written.

I was impressed by his intensity and seriousness though

I could not match them. Even at that young age his interests were wide, obsessive and inflexible. He could be explaining Schoenberg's twelve-tone row to you, his penetrating eyes demanding your attention; while you were listening you could see a cigarette end smouldering in his trouser's turn-up, yet you dare not interrupt his flow to point out the mishap for you knew he would feel it to be trivial and embarrassing. The total absence of frivolity and the single-mindedness were part of his attraction.

Over the next four years we met at symphony concerts, plays, the continental cinema, and at the coffee bars that were beginning to appear, offering meeting places for the young. Such cafés brightened the austerity of heavily-blitzed, postwar Hull and in their steamy interiors you could, for a small financial outlay, enjoy hours of intellectual discourse. Since leaving school, George had become an art student and I worked in offices but our mutual interest in books kept the friendship going.

When, at the age of eighteen, I emerged from Sutton House, many of my friends disappeared but George did not. In fact, after I had gone back to live with my folks, he became so persistent a visitor as to be almost one of the family. Every day he would appear at my door looking handsome and dapper and proffering sometimes a poem, always a bunch of flowers. I thought they were from his mother's garden but it transpired that he had gathered them from neighbouring gardens en route. I found his intensity, now it was focused on me, irresistible.

George and his family lived on the outskirts of Hull in a rented, 1930s semi-detached house, with a garden at front and back and a bathroom. Although they were financially much better off than my family, they were not good at managing money so in many ways their existence was more comfortless than ours.

George's maternal grandmother had come from Scotland to work as a fisher lass, following the herring shoals down from one coastal port to the next. Brutalizing work and rough companions had worn away her natural refinement and in early middle-age she settled down to a life of alcoholism in Hull. She lured her teenaged, illegitimate daughter, Jean, away from the safe conformity of her native Scottish fishing village in the hope that Jean would support her by finding work in a Hull fishhouse. But the girl married Albert, who was the son of a regular soldier and his Maltese wife. Albert had volunteered at the beginning of the First World War and had been drafted into a cavalry regiment. He had to falsify his age, being only sixteen at the time; since he was so small and slight, I bet he looked about twelve. What sort of cynics manned the recruitment offices, I wonder? He lived through every kind of hell the Western Front had to offer and returned in 1918, mustard-gassed but otherwise whole.

Albert Hartley then found a job on the St Andrew's Dock as a bobber (a fish porter who unloaded the catch from the ship's hold), and he and Jean produced a daughter and four sons of whom George was the youngest. In 1952 when I met the Hartleys, the older children – Albert, Joan and Ron – were married. Joan and Ron were busily engaged in becoming upwardly socially mobile; only Bob and George lived at home.

Bob was thirtyish and a misfit. Both he and George were angry young men who hated the narrowness of their lives and resented each other's presence in the house. Their frequent flare-ups acted as a catalyst to the simmering irascibility of others of the clan. When Bob was demobbed from the Royal Navy, his father found him a job working as a bobber with him and Albert. Poorly educated but artistically gifted, and having seen a bit of life in foreign ports, Bob loathed his job and was infuriated by the airs and graces of his younger brother, George, whom he felt to be more fortunate than himself. He was irritated by the fecklessness of his family, their shabby furniture (gimcrack stuff bought on credit) and their lack of style. The stormy progress of his passionate love affairs dominated the household, for he was jealous, possessive and overbearing.

55

George was very like Bob in temperament, but he had built some cultural resources which helped to mitigate his frustration, distance him from his family and provide him with a promising intellectual life. He had gone from school, without qualifications, to the local art college where he met young people from different backgrounds who discussed the books they read, wrote verse and fiction, painted pictures and made sculptures. Peter, the father of Laurien, was on the fringes of this crowd and, coming from similar backgrounds, he and George struck up a sympathetic, if somewhat competitive, friendship.

A typical weekday afternoon at the Hartley home would reveal Dad with Albert, who lived down Hessle Road with his wife Rene. Rene worked all day in a fruit-shop so, after his morning nap, Albert biked up to see his parents. Bobbers started work at one or two o'clock in the morning and so had much of the day free. (If you were a light sleeper, you could hear the sound of their clogs echoing down the streets in the early hours.) The two men would be hunched over a table spread with mugs of tea, an ashtray full of Old Holborn stubs and the sporting pages of the *Hull Daily Mail*. Nothing was allowed to interrupt the early afternoon ritual of picking out the 'osses (at the weekend they did the football pools as well). The radio played, permanently tuned to Radio Luxembourg, but no one seemed to feel that was an interruption since it jangled away continuously and was only turned off at bedtime. In the stone-floored veranda that led off the living-room and contained a gas stove, a sink and two doors (behind which were a coalhouse and a lavatory), George's mother presided over the steaming chip pan. She turned out scrumptious, golden brown, irregularly-shaped wedges which were a real treat for me. My mother did not own anything as up-to-date as a chip pan and, in any case, she disapproved of the end product. Apart from weekend suppertime treats, brought in by Harry, chips were for people with no standards and chips in the afternoon she would have viewed as the height of decadence.

Bob wore at least three clean white shirts a day, which he carefully inspected for smuts after his mother had ironed them. Bob saw himself as the poor man's version of one of his tough guy heroes – Frank Sinatra or Robert Mitchum. Frowning at the reflection, in the mirror over the mantelpiece, of his thinning fair hair, he would give his widow's peak a last smoothing flick and saunter off for a few lunchtime beers. If, by the time he had reached the top of the street, the wind was blowing in the wrong direction and had disarranged his hair, he would turn round, come back, puff furiously at his Players and raise hell.

Albert was the most solid, practical and least volatile member of the family. He was a dab hand at wallpapering and most other household jobs. Generous with his time and full of fun, Albert was often the peace-maker during family bust-ups, provided he got on to the scene before the frightened neighbours had called the police.

In 1953 George had left the art college and was working, temporarily as it turned out, at a smart shoe-shop in Hull. I was working temporarily at a rope manufacturers called Chisholm, Fox & Garner in order to get enough stamps on my insurance card to qualify for Maternity Benefit for I was pregnant again. Hindsight tells me I should have been reading Dr Marie Stopes rather than Ernest Dowson. We were both living with our respective parents and, at that time, Laurien was eighteen months old. George and I were twenty and considered to be 'courting' – as it used to be called.

One day Collett's, Hull's well-stocked leftwing book-shop started its closing-down sale and George bought a handful of greatly reduced literary magazines which would normally have been well beyond his price range. Being interested but unambitious, I read them merely for pleasure whereas George, who had a whim of iron, decided we should start a little magazine of our own and call it *Poetry Hull*. Let's be blatantly provincial, we thought. Chisholm, Fox & Garner's typewriter came in handy over the next couple of months as I typed begging letters to every poet we could think of. We also got in touch with Robin Skelton, a little-magazine editor at that time, and he was very helpful with suggestions and lists of names and addresses of possible subscribers.

Our confidence was as immense as our ignorance. I remember sitting at my four-quid-a-week job, with burgeoning belly clamped into deceiving corset and the boss safely on the telephone in the next room, writing to Ezra Pound at St Elizabeth's Hospital, Washington (we thought it must be a rest home):

Dear Mr Pound

I am starting a literary magazine to be called *Poetry Hull* although it is to be distributed nationally. It will contain the best of current poetry and criticism. I have long admired your work and would be grateful for any contribution you could make.

Yours sincerely,

George Hartley.

I began and ended, in true female tradition, as anonymous dogsbody except for the token 'business manager' credit from the fourth issue of the magazine onwards. My friend Audrey had married Eric Johnston, a man who was extremely knowledgeable about books and business. He had appeared as business manager in the first three issues. Subsequently, as I was immediately available to do most of the work, Eric, who had heavy family and work commitments, dropped into the background.

We found a local jobbing printer who was pleased, if somewhat nervous, to undertake the work. And we got married – a matter of less moment than the taking of the manuscript to the printers. We should have bought nappies or necessary household equipment with my accumulated back payment of child maintenance money – a windfall from Peter which came to the massive total of

£28 – but George had other ideas so we bought a cumbersome old Underwood typewriter and moved into 253 Hull Road, Hessle.

It was a tiny two-up-and-two-down, hundred-and-fifty-year-old, jerry-built workman's cottage, on the main road from Hull, with an outside lavatory, no bathroom, a cold-water tap in the kitchen, a shallow yellow stone sink and indoor slugs. I remember, a few years later, a literary lady looking round it in surprise and saying to me, 'How odd. I thought you would live in a large, rambling Victorian house' to which I replied, 'So did I.' The sale price of the house was £600. We had a private mortgage, with the owner of the property, and repaid it at the rate of £1 a week.

Before Alison was born, I asked my doctor if I could be booked into a maternity hospital. He looked surprised at such importunity. I explained that our house was primitive, the plumbing minimal, the heating facilities inadequate and that it was poorly equipped for a confinement. He brushed all this aside and said that I was lucky I had a roof over my head; didn't I think I was being rather selfish in wanting to take up a hospital bed? Easily squashed, I agreed that perhaps he was right. New Year's Day 1954 dawned cold and windy and my labour pains started. George dropped a note off at the midwife's house on his way to work and alerted his mother who had offered to come and help me. Together we filled all the available ironmongery – two pans, a kettle and a bucket – with water and put them on the gas cooker to boil. The midwife called, made an examination, decided I would be all right to leave for a few hours and announced that she was going back home for a kip. She had been at a New Year's Eve party and still felt hungover. After wheezing her way up our almost vertical staircase in order to check the bedroom, she frowned at the minuscule wrought-iron fireplace and told us to build a fire. The temperature upstairs was sub-zero; I don't suppose anyone had lit a fire there since the house was built. When she had gone George's mother and I got cracking and produced nothing but a roomful of smoke. After three attempts a dead bird fell out of the chimney and into the grate. We finally coaxed the fire into submission and after an hour or two the edge of the chill was taken off.

Alison was so reluctant to be born that I have often thought she must have had a preview of life and decided against it. When she did arrive, I was amazed by her skinny, chicken-wing legs, the shock of black hair and the dark eyes that looked as if they had been on this earth before. The midwife cradled her in a nappy, safety-pinned it to a balance and weighed her – four pounds twelve ounces. The midwife shook her head. 'Too small. Should be in hospital really. You must pack her round with hot water bottles and change them every two hours night and day for the next week.' Alison looked so fragile that I hardly dared touch her for fear she might break.

The magazine was born at the same time as Alison. By now, at my suggestion, George had changed its name to *Listen*. I sat up in bed, Alison in the cot beside me, Laurien tearing round the icy bedroom, and the Underwood on my knees, typing invoices to Brown's, Bowes & Bowes, Heffer's, Better Books, etc: '12 copies of *Listen* on sale or return.' That system works well for bookshops and it is fine if they sell and the money rolls in, but it is grim when dog-eared and unsaleable ones are returned.

Our London correspondents, Gordon Wharton and Stanley Chapman, had given us many helpful suggestions. Gordon supplied us with lists of subscribers to defunct little magazines and Stanley, a Pataphysician, dedicated Francophile and translator of the surrealist Boris Vian, apart from diverting us with his typographically inventive letters, designed our first cover: a striking black and white sun-face with a big, listening ear.

From Ezra Pound's kindly missive declining our invitation to contribute, we made a thrifty extraction. His letter had begun: 'Congrats on showing a spark of life in your distressed area.' We printed the last two lines: 'Birdie no sing in cage. Can I serve you in any other way? Cordially, E.P.' and placed them at the end of the magazine enclosed in a black border.

We did not grow more prosperous: less in fact. In February, when George was twenty-one, the shoe-shop sacked him rather than pay him the statutory increase due to him on having gained his majority. Peter, who was now living the bohemian life in London, had been ordered to pay me five shillings a week towards Laurien's upkeep but when he heard of my marriage to George, he wrote me a letter suggesting he should stop paying. My finer feelings told me just to forget the maintenance. So we were living on £4 a week unemployment benefit. Thin pickings for two adults and two children.

Six weeks after Alison was born, I went to the clinic for a post-natal examination. After the formalities of weighing and probing were over, I asked the apparently friendly female doctor about contraception. I have never seen anyone's face transformed so quickly, and I was frightened by the vehemence of her response: 'Why does a healthy young woman like you want to know about such things? You can have lots more fine babies. Don't ever mention that word again.' I rushed tearfully into the ante-chamber to put my clothes back on, feeling guilty and perplexed. I neither felt nor looked healthy. Two pregnancies in two years had left me with a prolapsed womb, varicose veins and gaps where three teeth used to be. I was underweight, too undernourished to breast feed and at twenty-one, looked at least ten years older. A kindly middle-aged attendant nurse appeared and mopped up my tears. As she scribbled on a piece of paper, she said to me, *sotto voce,* 'Take no notice of her, love. She's a Catholic. She's like that with everybody. Here's the address of the family planning clinic. You go and get yourself fixed up with a top hat.' I did just that and, once the means of preventing 'mistakes' were in my own hands, I made no more mistakes of that kind.

George's enforced idleness gave us more time together to think about and plan the second issue of *Listen*. With wider reading our tastes were beginning to change from a liking for the unashamedly romantic in both subject and style, to work by poets who, although not necessarily less romantic in outlook, were concerned with rigour of form and the achievement of a drier tone of voice. Our local printer, whose main work was the printing of raffle tickets and lolly wrappers, had risen admirably to the printing of *Listen* Vol. 1, No. 1, but, comparing it with other magazines, we could see that the margins were mean and the registration rocky.

We were excited by the innovations of the poets who were later to be collectively labelled 'The Movement' and so for our second issue, we wrote off to Philip Larkin, Donald Davie, A. Alvarez, Kingsley Amis, John Wain and others, spread ourselves to twenty-eight pages and a couple of book reviews, and asked Patrick Heron to design a cover for us. By now we had a new London printer – John Sankey of Villiers Publications – who taught us a great deal about paper, type founts and sizes, and explained the mysteries of printing. He specialized in the printing of little magazines and was interested in the contents as well as the aesthetics of production. He was also amazingly long-suffering about our delays in paying our bills.

The magazine thrived, critically at any rate, but I would recommend poetry publishing only to enthusiasts with private incomes and a penchant for proof-reading, bookkeeping, invoice typing and parcel wrapping. Taste and judgement are essential, of course, and you will soon know if you have those qualities by the number of orders and the tenor of the letters and reviews you receive. The interesting bit, the editorial work, is a small part of the enterprise – it bears the same relation to production as conception does to pregnancy. Nor, if you live in the provinces, are your authors likely to come to see you, so you are deprived of that bit of glamour. Only Americans will venture, their rationale mystifying to an islander: 'I was in Italy on a Fulbright so I guessed I'd just run over to see you.'

Running a little magazine with no mod.cons. (we did not have a telephone until 1960) involved me in endless routine work. The post would thump through the door each morning: an avalanche of poems, fan letters, orders from bookshops, subscriptions with cheques, postal orders or sometimes a few dollar bills. The processing of all this correspondence had to be fitted in between running a labour-intensive house and looking after a family. From as far back as I can remember, I had wanted to live the literary life, but being poetry's midwife-cum-charwoman was not quite what I had envisaged.

Seven

By the end of 1954, with three issues of *Listen* behind us, George felt that he would like to publish a book. Knowing that most of the work would fall on me, I was not so keen but any protest I might have made would have been both useless and painful. I felt that our priority should have been to earn some instant money and drag ourselves out of the poverty trap. To me, fine book productions were not much consolation when we had no winter clothes, the children were clad in darned passed-ons and there was often not enough food to eat. It is ironical that George, whose will was centred on higher matters than overcoming the material hardships, is now – in consequence – a prosperous man.

The second issue of *Listen* had included Philip Larkin's 'Spring', 'Dry-point' and 'Toads' and his 'Poetry of Departures' was in the third issue which had gone to press. This handful of poems, with their accessibility, wide range of mood and rare combination of wit, lyricism and disenchantment, excited us more than anything else we had been offered, so he was our obvious first choice and we wrote to ask him if he had enough poems to form a collection to inaugurate The Marvell Press. We chose the name because of the local association with Andrew Marvell – and the fact that it would be a bloody marvel if we did manage to publish a book.

Philip's reply came from Queen's University, Belfast, and was encouraging. He would accept our offer provided it didn't cost him anything and provided we made a good job of it. He announced he had been given the post of Librarian at Hull University and that he would be coming across to Hull in March 1955, when we might meet to discuss the matter further. He expressed nervousness about being published so near to what would become his home, his poems being 'nothing if not personal'.

We were, at that time, dimly aware that there was a university in Hull but our acquaintance with it was limited to my attendance there at some of Richard Hoggart's WEA literature classes. We reassured Philip that we had absolutely no links with Hull University and that our magazine *Listen* sold scarcely any copies locally. Brown's, the largest Hull bookshop, had been pressed into taking a few but, in the event of Philip letting us publish his book, we were quite prepared to forego any sales there.

Although initially he had been content to leave discussion of a projected collection until his arrival in Hull, by the following month we received a postcard which revealed his growing enthusiasm for the idea. He promised to send about twenty-five poems for inspection, though again he expressed his distaste at the thought of any link between his profession as a librarian and his life as a poet: 'the man who creates and the man who suffers.'

With his next letter he enclosed a collection of poems, the backbone of which was the privately printed XX Poems (1951). He had sent this out to a number of literati but received no response. He put this down to the fact that he had posted them with penny stamps shortly after the printed paper rate had gone up to a penny ha'penny. What an unLarkin-like oversight! This incident is very wittily documented in his potted history of *The Less Deceived* which appears on the first sleeve of *The Less Deceived* record; not to be confused with the second sleeve for which, in a disarming imaginary interview, he gave his views on reading poetry and, incidentally, made a naughty reference to one of the more awkward moments of our relationship. He speaks of an occasion when George and I were sitting on a settee with Philip wedged cosily between us. Without warning, George thrust in front of Philip a nakedly personal love peom, dedicated to me and extremely long. When Philip reached the bottom of the page he thought he had come to the end and sat trapped, silent and embarrassed at being put on the spot. Philip tried desperately to find something to say but nothing leapt to mind. After what seemed like an eternity, George said, encouragingly: 'It goes on over the page,' and Philip comments, 'It did, too.'

We were, of course, thrilled to receive his collection – a ragbag assortment printed on different sizes of paper, some quarto typescript and others cut out of the various magazines and pamphlets in which they had first appeared. The instructions that went with the collection however, showed what we later realized was a characteristic Larkin scrupulousness and a meticulous attention to detail. He had, for example, used roman numerals to mark the order in which the poems were to be printed, giving page numbers in arabic at the foot.

In his next letter Philip thanked us for sending him the latest issue of *Listen*, Vol. 1 No. 3. He praised Kingsley Amis's contribution adding that he felt anything written by Kingsley seemed to him original and distinguished. He admired Jonathan Price's poem, and was surprised to find himself liking Tom Scott's 'A Ballat o Fat Margie' (after Villon). This was a rumbustious piece of Scottish dialect bawdry, not dissimilar in vein to 'The Card Players' (in *High Windows*), Philip's own later venture into the grotesque. He was somewhat scathing, however, of Robin Skelton's favourable review of Norman Nicholson's *The Pot Geranium*, although he conceded that everyone had sex appeal for someone, poetically speaking, anyway.

In sending Philip *Listen* No. 3, we had told him of the host of enthusiastic letters we had received about his poem 'Toads', which had appeared in the second issue. He was pleased about this as he felt that he had 'really expressed something of the great heart of the people'. The toad creature was an inspired choice as an emblem for work, and the poem's debate shows the powerful inner conflict felt by most people who accept and need the work habit but feel trapped by it: work displaces a huge portion of life and inhibits spontaneity and daring.

Eager to dissociate ourselves from its provinciality, we warned Philip that Hull was the armpit of the East Riding. We expressed surprise that he should want to come and work in the place from which we had failed to escape. Of course we did not understand what a large career stride the move represented for him, nor did we know anything about the man himself and his essentially reclusive nature. He told us that he had also been warned that Belfast was drab and dull, yet his five years there had been very happy ones. What he liked about a town was smallness, proximity of countryside, friendly people and a feeling of being cut off from the mainstream. He did not particularly care for a rich cultural life and could live without theatres, concerts and poetry readings. So he felt that Hull might be more to his taste than we thought.

By February 1955, as the time for leaving approached, his letters to us revealed the doubts of a man who has taken two irrevocable decisions and, at the last minute, wonders why. His move from the post of Sub-Librarian at Belfast University to that of Librarian at Hull would entail a great deal more work and responsibility. He had also entrusted his precious manuscript to a novice publishing firm to experiment with and present to the poetry-reading public. (For all he knew, he might be in for a repeat performance of his unhappy Fortune Press experience.) The thought of leaving Belfast was threatening to crush his spirit, and was preventing him from writing poetry. Ireland, now he was leaving it, had suddenly become more attractive to him.

Philip arrived in Hull in March 1955, and in fact the town suited him admirably, as can be seen in his celebratory poem, 'Here', in which he sees mid-'50s Hull as a mosaic of opposites: potentially romantic in its setting, grand civic buildings and unusual occupations, but peopled by the practical working classes whose horizons are narrowed by the town's isolation. The shape of the poem mirrors the idea of a train journey from country through town to country again and shows Hull surrounded by lushness and rich countryside running off to nothing at Spurn Point. Economically using hyphenated double adjectives to give visual fulness to the nouns, he captures exactly the romantic yet prosaic quality of the place, eschewing metaphor as, presumably, a device too fanciful to describe the mundane town and its inhabitants.

Hull in 1955 was dotted with empty spaces and piles of bricks and rubble for, like Coventry, Philip's home-town, it had suffered from heavy wartime bombings. Nevertheless, Hull still retained some riches. On the river front was the two-tiered, wooden pier – a fine goal for families' Sunday walks. Their children larked about on the superstructure, scaring themselves by peeping at the water through the cracks between the planks. It was also an excellent vantage point for looking across the two miles or so of river to the ferry terminal at New Holland. As a child I thought this must be a foreign country. On the left of the pier was the horse wash – still used in 1955. On the right was the ferry-boat ticket office and the gangplank which led to the steamer. On some evenings in summer, local jazz bands were hired to play for a Riverboat Shuffle and the voices of boozy revellers would ring out over the dark waters. The pier was later demolished and, although the ferry still had a purpose to serve, it was closed in 1981 as soon as the Humber Bridge opened.

Clerical workers walking to their offices in the old town had to pass over Monument Bridge – named after the monument to William Wilberforce which once stood there – and on their left they would see the Queen of the Waterworks, a statue of the costive-looking Victoria raised aloft over the municipal lavatories. To the right was Prince's

Dock, which invariably held three or four ships awaiting repair. My father and brother worked for the large marine engineering firm that blazoned its advertising sign above the ship funnels; at that time, the unremitting noise issuing from the wet and dry docks proclaimed the industry's healthy state. The Cod Wars and the general decline in the shipping industry in the 1970's left Princes Dock empty and silent for many years. Now a giant shopping centre and car park squat there on stilts. It nudges us into conformity with other big northern towns. Other industries such as fishing and seed-crushing, which flourished in 1955 and provided much employment, have since disappeared and with them has gone much of the quaintness that Philip noticed, not to mention the prosperity.

In the centre of the town a dock – once the biggest of its kind in England – had, in 1934, been filled in and made into a park known as Queen's Gardens. In 1955 it was an irregular area of grassy hummocks, with a random assortment of trees and flowerbeds, adorned with a bandstand and a majestic fountain. In the 1960s it was landscaped into a neat regularity that is only now, two decades later, beginning to soften. The College of Further Education stretches across one end of these gardens and, from its seventh floor, you can look across the grass and trees to the gleaming copper domes of the civic buildings beyond it and imagine you are in Kiev.

Within the figtree-covered walls of the Slave Museum (Wilberforce House) gardens you are, at high tide, on a level with the swaying barges which line up where the mouth of the River Hull opens on to the wide estuary of the Humber. Most of the Elizabethan and Georgian buildings that still graced the town in 1955 have been demolished, replaced by glass-and-concrete office blocks and supermarkets but, at the time when Philip was writing 'Here', there was much to appeal to a poet who valued Hull's variety and remoteness.

For his collection Philip provisionally chose the title

69

Various Poems. Neither he nor we thought it a very arresting title, but the virtue he claimed for it was that no poet had used it for at least ten years. We were keen to make the collection as substantial as possible and asked him if we could include additional poems such as 'Spring' and 'No Road'. Philip had felt these two poems were a bit below the general standard but he allowed us to convince him of their worthiness.

He took great care over the order in which the poems were placed and explained that his aim was to make the tone as various as possible – in harmony with the title – by alternating poems with different atmospheres and styles rather than keeping the mood level and grouping similar poems together. He also used this method of arrangement in *Whitsun Weddings* and *High Windows*. During the months in which the book was in preparation, Philip was still amending odd words or phrases such as replacing 'early days' with 'first few days' in 'Maiden Name' and then substituting 'fine clear days'. He finally reverted to 'first few days' on the grounds that 'fine clear days' sounded too much like a BBC weather report.

We were gratified by Philip's interest in the technicalities of the book's production and its format. He had written that he did not mind us printing two short poems on one page but when he realized that we did not intend to stint on space and were prepared to splurge out on one poem per page, he was very pleased. Undecided about the two type-faces our printer had offered, we asked Philip, who told us he preferred Garamond to Bodoni.

Although nothing if not business-like, Philip was clearly not expecting to make any money from the book. I think he imagined that we would print a bijou edition of three hundred copies, that they would sell very gradually over the years and that perhaps in time the printing costs would be covered. We had in mind five hundred, which we thought of as a modest edition though our advisers cautioned us that it would be two hundred too many. We would all have laughed at the notion of selling several thousands of copies of the book, of selections from it being included in almost every anthology of modern verse, or the poems being translated into many foreign languages.

Philip's last letter to us before we met asked tentatively about what size of first edition we planned to print and delicately raised the point that if the book should prove popular enough to be kept in print, he would want to suggest some definite terms for a second printing, although he felt this last eventuality was most unlikely.

This nudged us into thinking about a contract, though neither he nor we imagined there would be any real need for one. We were keen to do the thing properly, so I drafted out a contract containing all the standard clauses but giving Philip a half share of the profit rather than the usual ten or twelve per cent of the price of the copies sold. Our offer was based on self-preservation rather than altruism since, if only three hundred sold we would be stuck with a huge bill from printer and binder, plus the royalty to Philip. In later years Philip often commented to me on the generosity of the contract and the gratifying additional income it gave him. Since we did not charge for our time or labour, Philip received the maximum half share. We tried very hard to get him to include an option on his next book but he would not budge. Natural caution, and having twice been bitten by The Fortune Press, who had published *Jill* and *The North Ship*, made him adamant about keeping his options open.

Later, he made it quite clear to us that, irrespective of any success we might have with *The Less Deceived*, he would want to offer any subsequent collection of poems first to Faber. In 1947 they had published his novel, *A Girl in Winter* and he had, quite reasonably, expected that they would take his collection of poems, *In the Grip of Light*. Their rejection of this book in 1948 undoubtedly dismayed him but, in the intervening fifteen years between that rejection and their acceptance of *The Whitsun Weddings*, it did

71

not sway him from his conviction that Faber and Faber was his spiritual home. He maintained a correspondence and friendship with their director, Charles Monteith, and kept his sights firmly fixed on Russell Square.

Eight

About a month after we received Philip's last letter from
Ireland we met him. Knowing his nature, I do not suppose
he was any less nervous about our first encounter than we
were. We had often speculated about his appearance and I
had decided he would have lots of ginger hair and a merry
smile with a hint of sadness round the eyes, and he would
have a liking for houndstooth jackets and green trousers. If
ours was not a typical publishing house, we were certainly
an unlikely pair of publishers. George was a small, handsome youth whose black hair and olive skin revealed his
Maltese ancestry. His insecurity betrayed itself in an odd
mixture of brash confidence and reserve whereas, on such
testing occasions, I tended to gush and be over-anxious to
please.

We felt self-conscious about the Marvell Press premises.
Our house stood in a row of twelve, next door to an off-
licence on one side and four doors away from a fried-fish
shop on the other. It was mean and cramped inside and its
horsehair-and-plaster walls efficiently relayed every sound
from the adjoining houses. At weekends we heard Alice
Turner at the beer-off practising scales with her piano
pupils, and Trev Deasle, a motor mechanic, using his
power tools to transform his property into a little palace.
At night he and Doris played over and over again the three
records they had bought on their wedding day: 'Shrimp
Boat', 'Jezebel' and 'White Christmas'. From outside, the
cottage looked passable with its tiny bay window and

minuscule garden. I planted fuchsia sprigs, to discourage the neighbourhood dogs from trespassing and when in blossom they looked quite pretty, once I had removed the grey fish-skins which the high-spirited fish shop customers nightly draped over them.

I had cleaned and titivated the house, hidden all the children's paraphernalia and tried to make the place look as arty as possible to disguise the furnishing deficiencies, but it can only have given an impression of extreme poverty – which might just have been mistaken for deliberate bohemianism, but I doubt it. Philip's diaries, which were destroyed after his death, would have revealed the misgivings he would undoubtedly have had when we opened the door of our hovel, and he thought 'how young' and we thought 'how old'. The difference between twenty-two and thirty-two seems enormous to people of those ages.

I was greatly alarmed when I saw a dignified gent, slim, with dark hair (receding), very formally-suited, serious and quite unsmiling. His frequent 'White Rabbit' glances at his pocket-watch did nothing to put us at our ease. It was hard to connect his solemn appearance with the wit of 'Toads' or the passion of 'Wedding Wind'. With his chin well tucked in he paced up and down our small living-room, his tall body bowed to avoid a head-on collision with the light bulb.

He later told me that this was a very lonely period in his life so perhaps it was partly for that reason, as well as our shared interest in literature and his desire to be involved in the production of his book, that he became a regular visitor. Most Saturdays he would come bowling along on his enormous bike (featured in the TV Monitor programme), the biggest I have ever seen, looking more than life-size as he pedalled down Hull Road, Hessle. On arrival, he would unhitch a huge haversack in which were the week's groceries that he had just bought in Hammond's food basement. One day a woman in front of him accidentally knocked over and smashed half a dozen jars of

74

jam, and Philip worried about what he would have done had it been he who had knocked them over. Anxiousness came easily to him, and fear of death was a subject which featured frequently in his conversation, but his unpretentiousness and self-mockery stopped him from ever seeming morbid or self-dramatising. He asked me if I was afraid of death. I said no, in fact it would be a happy release. This was a fairly accurate indicator of my state of mind at the time. He laughed, but clearly did not believe me.

We would talk about jazz, the progress of his book, the triumphs or setbacks of the week, who had just published what, and the price of meat. He was a marvellous mimic and his parodies of other poets were wickedly funny.

Memories of his treatment by Caton of The Fortune Press, who had published *The North Ship* and *Jill* and not paid him a penny, were never far from Philip's mind even though, characteristically, he had turned the episode into a joke. Therefore, unprepossessing though our outfit was, I think it was a comfort to him to have his new publisher living just down the road. It also gave him a chance to have a hand in the book's production. Together we discussed type sizes and faces, pagination, blurb, binding, and agreed on a lovely strong pink, his favourite colour, for the dust-jacket. Appreciating that we were broke, he asked me if I would like to type a clean copy of the book to submit to the printer, and he paid me £20 for the job. I was relieved to find that the only mistake I had made was the omission of one comma.

I think he had been feeling very gloomy about his publication prospects prior to receiving our offer. We were amazed to learn that many publishers, including Faber, had turned down a smaller collection he had submitted to them. When we said disbelievingly, 'You mean they rejected it?' he replied, 'Well, if you can call squashing a ripe tomato against a wall, rejecting it, yes.' Later, a small Irish firm, the Dolmen Press, had expressed an interest in his work but subsequently ran into money problems and they also rejected it. These disappointments and the pratfall of *XX Poems* had resigned him to seeing his work published only in anthologies and little magazines.

Having no money, and therefore no money problems, we decided to revive an eighteenth-century practice and to publish *The Less Deceived* by subscription, sending out forms to possible subscribers and printing their names as a roll of honour at the back of the first edition. This would give us some cash in hand to pay part of the printer's bill in the frightening lull between the book being reviewed, bookshops placing orders and the money actually rolling in. We had all our *Listen* subscribers to call on and Philip, then living temporarily at Holtby House, a male students' hall of residence, supplied us with what he was happy to call his 'sucker-list', containing the names and addresses of fifty suckers. This was added to from time to time over the next few months as he remembered the names and checked the addresses of more friends and admirers. Philip particularly asked us to keep the list for reference, presumably so that he could later check up on who his real friends were. He tentatively suggested we make provision on the subscription form for people to buy more than one copy; many of them did.

By the middle of April Philip had almost completed the titling of poems, which had originally only borne numbers. In deciding to call the Mayhew poem 'The Less Deceived', he toyed with the idea of using this as a title for the book, although if he did that he would have to find another title for the poem. He felt that to give the poem and the book the same title would draw too much attention to the poem and give too much emphasis to one mood. He relished the thought of his readers hunting through *Hamlet* to find Ophelia's words 'I was the more deceived' in response to Hamlet's 'I loved you not' and thought that this echo would suggest the flavour of the collection. Its resonance for me is that of Hardy's 'He never expected much'. Philip's ruminations over the title reveal an interesting contradiction in a poet who claimed that he detested the kind of poetry that leant on literary allusion. For a man who had steeped himself in books from an early age the literary pun came as naturally as breathing and proved irresistible.

Working on the book and looking forward to its publication gave him a necessary point of focus during these early days in Hull when he was gipsying from one lodging to another and, at the same time, working on plans for an ambitious expansion to the University library. The University itself was, in a sense, new, having been a University College until 1954, when it achieved university status.

In turn, we were glad to have his company. Our life seemed very circumscribed compared to the lives of our more ambitious friends who had left Hull. Frank Redpath was living in a bedsit in Notting Hill Gate. Its cafés were meeting places for people who did temporary jobs in the daytime and put the cultural and political worlds to rights in the evenings – or vice versa if they happened to work night shifts. Steve Ramsey's aptitude for languages had landed him a job as Continental traffic inspector at Liverpool Street Station, where he dealt with the day-to-day problems of travellers of all nationalities. Joyce and Steve's consequent move to the south of England cut off for me an important lifeline. My brother also felt the need to widen his horizons. He tried at first to emigrate to New Zealand on a government passage-paid scheme but New Zealand did not appear to need wood pattern-makers so he decided to go under his own steam and take any kind of job he could get.

Those of our friends who still lived in Hull were mostly single, building careers and having a good time socially. Trapped by what we had chosen – marriage and children – we could do none of these things. What we did was to argue a lot. Our personalities were incompatible and the most trivial matter could spark off a row. The perennial bone was the electric slot meter. It was my job (what wasn't?) to make sure that we always had enough shillings to replenish the electricity meter. But being human and over-worked, it happened that, at least once a week, we would be plunged into darkness just as dusk had fallen or at 10.30 p.m when George was emphasising some important point to a literary visitor. The visitor would make some polite remark about blown fuses, whereupon I would light a candle, apologetically explain our archaic lighting system and search my pockets. If this failed, my next step was to nip out to the bus-stop, flag down the first bus that approached, and return victorious to hear George, who was the most easily embarrassed person I have ever known, holding forth in the unacknowledged darkness on, say, *Seven Types of Ambiguity,* as if no interruption had occurred. After the visitor's departure, it was another story.

Earlier in the year we had had the truly Gargantuan electric slot meter crisis. Christmas 1954 had been frugal but peaceful, and we had much to be thankful for. Alison had survived a serious bout of gastroenteritis and Albert had helped us to decorate both living-rooms. One night, at eight o'clock, just after New Year, as I was getting the children ready for bed, the light went out and, since I was fastening a nappy, George agreed to go in search of a shilling. Half an hour went by and he had not returned. It was both frustrating and frightening to be sitting in the dark, unable to get on with anything, and the children were fretful. I began to worry and after half an hour I fumbled about, put both children in the pram and walked to Hessle Square, peering blindly in every direction (my glasses had been broken a few months earlier). Being an alarmist, I felt sure George must be dead in a ditch somewhere since the shilling search seldom took longer than ten minutes.

On the way back I popped into the still darkened house to check – no George – and so tramped off in the opposite direction to George's parents' house hoping I might find him there. But they too were mystified as to where he could be. Just as I had decided to go back home, Bob came in. He had had an argument with his girl-friend in the pub so he walked out and left her there. On learning about my predicament he suggested I stay and have a cup of tea while he walked down to 253 to investigate. As he lurched off into the night, I had an uneasy feeling that the plan was not a wise one but it is difficult to argue with a man who has been drinking and by now I had reached the 'sod it all' stage and was happy to let the Hartley family take over. It was cosy sitting there by the fire with the children asleep in the pram, but as time went by and Bob did not return I grew restive and anxious. I got up to go but George's father said I should stay and that he would pedal down to see what was what. It was about eleven o'clock by this time and my imagination was running riot: perhaps the Hessle teddy boys had waylaid George. How would I manage as a widow with two children?

Within ten minutes George's father was back. He burst in foaming at the mouth with excitement and anger. 'You'd better get back there quick. They've half killed each other and it's all your bloody fault, you stupid cow. Our Bob was only sticking up for you. Why couldn't you just sit tight and wait for George to come back? He'd only gone next door but one.' I could never understand why I was always nominated the central role in the upheavals when, to me, I only ever seemed to be on the periphery.

I ran home, pushed through the knot of spectators and opened the front door. Blood streaked the walls that had been newly papered a couple of weeks earlier. Both glass doors were shattered, household objects lay littered about in confusion and the toy pram my parents had bought Laurien for Christmas was a twisted jumble of scrap metal. George sat drinking tea amid the wreckage. He had the beginnings of a black eye and some cuts and bruises. Bob was nowhere to be seen.

The story was that Bob had been sitting in the darkened house when George returned with the shilling. The neighbour had kept him talking and, unthinkingly, he had stayed for three hours or so to hear her life story and be given a guided tour of the house. When he walked in he was startled to hear Bob asking him, unceremoniously, where he had been. George replied that it was none of Bob's business. Bob countered by saying that it was his business, that I was out of my mind with worry and that he considered George's treatment of me was abominable. At this, the resentment that had been smouldering in both of them must have caught fire and a fight began. Bob, encouraged by Hull Brewery bitter, struck the first blow and after that it became a free for all using every object that came to hand. In turn they pushed each other through a glass door (a popular household sport at 253; every few months Albert came and measured up for a new pane). As they gravitated nearer to the front door, a neighbour called the police. George's father appeared just as Bob, bleeding copiously from the head, was being carted off in an ambulance to have his wound stitched. I surveyed the ruins and wondered how I had come to find myself in the middle of an Emile Zola novel and how I could disguise the truth from my parents.

Philip's visits were pleasant islands of civility dotted between what were often seas of discontent. Occasionally when he called, if the weather was fine, we would all go for a walk. One lovely warm Saturday we walked along the Hessle foreshore to Ferriby, about five miles there and back. Walking parallel to the railway line, we passed a row of old cottages, their gardens heavy with the scents of jasmine, carnation and honeysuckle. A black, derelict windmill guarded the entrance to Little Switzerland, at one time a quarry but now a wilderness of bramble with clearings of wild strawberries and chalky pools over which insects hummed continually. Further on was the rank-smelling Corporation dump where, from discarded kitchen rubbish, tomatoes and sunflowers had seeded themselves and begun to reclaim the land. Halfway there Alison began to flag, so Philip gave her a piggy-back the rest of the way. The river bank has been altered now by the building of the Humber Bridge, but then it presented a remote and open vista with sheep straying across the path. The sound of a bell-buoy hung in the air. Great stretches of bird-marked mud-flats edged the chalky path and, as we walked, we looked out at the endless space where 'sky and Lincolnshire and water meet'.

For me, having always lived at the western side of the city, the walk we were taking was a much-loved one. That day the river was looking its best and I felt pleased to be able to show the familiar view to a newcomer. Philip was clearly enchanted with the day and the sense that we were part of an endless canvas painted in horizontal bands of misty blue, muted green and palest lemon. He grew to love the river in all its different moods, from turbulent to level calm. From the bank on a dull day it can appear a flat, steely grey but seen from a boat and lit by the setting sun its rich browns seem set with peacock blue scales. One winter it was a mass of floating frozen slabs. Each year it exacts a human tribute, for its constantly shifting sand-banks and fast-flowing tidal races make it one of the most unpredictable and dangerous estuaries in the world. Passing the Humber by train, on journeys into or out of town, I never fail to catch my breath at first sight of this immense stretch of water. The image nourished many of the poems Philip wrote during his life in Hull. It appears early on: the first stanza of 'Here' and lines from 'The Whitsun Weddings', and again in later poems such as 'Livings' and the cantata *A Bridge for the Living*.

Arriving at Ferriby, we had a drink on a bench outside the Duke of Cumberland while the girls played on the grass. When George went to buy another round, Philip made a dry remark about what an unexpected pleasure it was to have his publisher buy him a drink. He was not to know that, notwithstanding George's natural parsimony, the tight household budget did not allow for beer. On the way back Philip entertained us with shockingly ribald parodies of great poets. One of his best was a version of Hardy's 'Afterwards' which listed all sorts of dubious activities and retained the punchline 'He was a man who used to notice such things.'

Friendly correspondence with one of the contributors to *Listen*, Martin Seymour-Smith, brought an invitation to visit him and his wife, Janet. They had recently returned from Majorca where Martin had tutored Robert Graves's son, William, and Janet, a classics scholar, had helped with Graves's *Greek Myths*. We spent a delightful weekend with them in their rented, fourteenth-century Sussex cottage, which had an earthen ground floor, different levels upstairs and twisting passages; reading poetry, drinking Rioja, listening to their Deyá reminiscences, and to the Spanish folk-pop records they had brought back. A wild scheme of driving to Brighton, in relays, on Martin's motor-bike was broached from time to time but, a little disappointingly, inertia saved us.

I was struck by the difference between southern, commuter-filled villages – the houses expensively restored or tarted up with fake bottle-glass, and the cavalry-twilled inhabitants moneyed and snooty, not a peasant to be seen – and northern villages, which suffered a similar transfiguration but not until a decade later and, even so, never achieved the twee pretentiousness of their southern counterparts.

This visit paved the way for a subsequent invitation to Martin's parents' house in Finchley. Martin and Janet's finances were at a low ebb, so they decided to try to restore the balance and save on rent and household expenses by giving up housekeeping for a while. Janet was staying with her parents and Martin and the two girls with his parents – Miranda was about four years old and Charlotte two. Martin's mother wanted to get away from Finchley for a breather so it was suggested that we might stay there for a holiday and help with the children. George arranged to sign on at the same Labour Exchange as Martin, and they rattled around London together visiting, I suspect, as many pubs as their pockets would permit. I think that, officially, they were looking for jobs or making literary connections and one day, when they had slipped off to The White City, Martin's father Frank asked me where they were. Not appreciating the delicate position, I answered innocently, 'They've gone to the dogs.' Frank looked very disapproving and when they appeared he challenged them with what I'd said. 'No, of course we haven't', Martin answered. 'Jean was speaking metaphorically.'

The three of us were in awe of the stately Frank, who had in his younger days been a gifted and innovative librarian. He now worked for W. H. Smith, for whose offices he departed, dark-suited and bowler-hatted, each morning. His assumption that his own high standards would be universally shared, and the seriousness of his manner, made me feel that all household matters should be just-so when he returned in the evenings. But they seldom were. I was never a strong disciplinarian and I felt too much of an interloper to be more than tentative in re-proving someone else's children. Miranda, much more high-spirited and assertive than my own daughters, was at the book-tearing stage and Charlotte was not quite house-trained. My cooking was embryonic and I felt nervous in a strange kitchen. I wilted as Frank brought in a precious tome from the garden and gloomily displayed pages which had been ravaged and rained on. However, he pitched in and tried to raise the level of domestic management. It was, of course, easier for him to chivvy his son than to criticize me or George. His always dignified intonations could be heard calling 'Martin! Are you aware that Charlotte has just soiled her shorts?' Or in the morning, when Martin was still enjoying morning-after sleep, his clear call would ring out, 'Martin! If you do not come down now, your kipper will be quite dry and valueless.'

Frank was a good cook and he brought back from town exotic vegetables I had never seen before: aubergines, courgettes and shiny red, green and yellow peppers – at that time readily available on London market stalls but still scarce in the provinces, and only to be found in the poshest greengroceries. I shall be eternally grateful to him for the lessons I learned in his kitchen, while watching him create spicy, continental, peasant-style dishes. When the children were asleep, Frank would reward us by playing some of his treasured old 78 r.p.m. records. Once he played Beethoven's *Hammerclavier* about which he felt so passionate that, during the most moving passages, he put the light out to remove all other sensory distractions. I am ashamed to say that George, Martin and I refused to rise to the sacredness of the occasion and giggled and nudged each other like naughty third-formers whenever his hand hit the light switch. After he had gone to bed, the three of us sat up drinking beer, and talking poetry and personalities late into the night.

Nine

Philip Larkin's collection was taking its final shape. Though it was still a slim volume when at last it was printed, we had persuaded Philip to include many more poems than he had originally anticipated. 'Born Yesterday', the poem addressed to Sally Amis which had been published in *The Spectator,* was a late inclusion. Philip felt that although it was slight, Kingsley might be annoyed if he left it out, especially as he intended to dedicate his book not to Kingsley but to Monica Jones. He thought Kingsley might have been expecting him to make a reciprocal gesture as he had dedicated *Lucky Jim* to Philip, thereby taking his name into a million households.

Always sensitive to noise, Philip was finding the radio at his new digs a nuisance; it helped, but not much, to stuff his ears with cotton-wool from an aspirin bottle. The house had advantages over the hall of residence, his previous berth, where loutish research students had played games of passage–soccer using a rubber bulb from a motor horn. But the radio annoyed him so much that he declared he would like to build a public convenience for camels over the grave of Signor Marconi. He himself was not entirely blameless in the matter of noise pollution. When he eventually moved to Pearson Park, the other tenants in the house were regularly regaled with the raucous jazz numbers that emanated from his record player. I suppose most of us are guilty of such paradoxical intolerance and self-indulgence.

Philip at last decided to call the Mayhew poem 'Deceptions', leaving *The Less Deceived* free for the title of the collection. He felt *The Less Deceived* would be fitting in that it was not ambiguous and made no claims of policy or belief. He also thought it gave a 'certain impression of sad-eyed (and clear-eyed) realism' and that if readers picked up the Hamlet context, it would give them an insight into his basic passivity as regards poetry and life. Philip felt that the doer of any act is always more deceived than the passive recipient of an act. For the doer acts from desire which comes from unfulfilled wants but when these wants are fulfilled they do not necessarily bring happiness. Whereas, Philip claimed, there was absolutely no deception involved in suffering: 'no one *imagines* they're suffering'. His point was that, although in conventional terms it would not seem to be so, the raped girl in the poem 'Deceptions' was less deceived than the rapist, whose expectations met only with 'fulfilment's desolate attic.'

That summer, after being unemployed for many months, George took a job as a windowdresser with Austin Reed, the gents' outfitters. They sent him down to London for what he was told would be a six-weeks training course at the Red Lion Square branch but, being short-staffed over the holiday period, they kept him there for four months. It gave him the chance to meet many of the writers with whom we had corresponded and, as my cousins Joyce and Steve Ramsey were putting him up, I was able to join him for a week's holiday. My parents looked after the children.

Joyce and Steve were not at all sure about George. In Hull he had seemed to be irritating and sometimes supercilious but, after all, he had Stuck By Me, as they say; we were buying our own house, *Listen* was being produced, a book was in the pipeline and, as far as they knew, I was happy with him. Still, it was not really the best of times for them to take George in. They were renting a primitive railway-owned house at the end of a cul-de-sac off Vallance Road, Bethnal Green (later to become notorious because of its connections with the Kray brothers) and struggling with the housing problems of London in 1955, to find a house they could afford to buy. Joyce, who worked for the L.C.C. was in the early stages of pregnancy. Still, George's stay would only be for six weeks, so they thought; Paul would be in Scarborough with his grandmother for the summer holidays and George could have his bedroom.

As the six weeks stretched to four months, there arose the problem of the guest who outstays his welcome. George kept his literary life quite separate from his Austin Reed and Bethnal Green lives; nevertheless his presence in the cramped Ramsey household was palpable. He had to be nagged to get up and out in the mornings and reminded to send money home to me as soon as he got paid. When Paul, aged twelve, arrived back from Scarborough, his first thought was: so this is how a poet lives, sitting by the fireplace in the best chair, feet on the mantelpiece, listening to the Third Programme and dropping his cigarette ash on the floor in neat little piles – just like rabbit droppings.

Joyce was impressed by George's talents: he wrote poetry instead of talking about it, he painted and sculpted and he knew what was going on in the literary world. He also spent a great deal of time with John Sankey, the printer, meticulously going over the details of the forthcoming Larkin publication. One day a cheque for £28 arrived – royalties from the Third Programme. Joyce was delighted and translated it immediately in her mind into shoes and other clothes for me and the children but George said that it was *Listen* money and not for spending.

George was very concerned with appearances. I was vetted from head to foot before he would walk out of the door with me. Facial expressions of joy, anguish, dismay or whatever, were vetoed because they would produce lines on my face. There were times when I could scarcely get through half a sentence without: 'You're pulling that face again.' On family photographs we were not to smile, and I still have collections of holiday snapshots of the four of us looking like refugees from *The Grapes of Wrath*. During the week that I stayed in London, when the heatwave was well into its stride, George promised to introduce me to our printer. I had very few clothes and the only outfit George approved of was a polo-necked, long-sleeved, black woollen jumper, a green skirt and black, stiletto-heeled shoes. To keep the peace, I wore it and sweated miserably through the entire baking hot day.

Even the frozen north suffered from the excruciating heat that August. A letter Philip wrote to George in London dwelt on it and on how uncomfortable his living conditions were. He grumbled that almost any kind of food went bad within half an hour of its purchase in the heat. This reminded me that in 1955 not one person I knew owned a fridge.

Philip called to see me and together we went through *The Less Deceived* subscription slips which were beginning to fill a shoebox. Pre-publication excitement was mounting, and the fact that already we had over a hundred subscribers consoled Philip for all the reviews Kingsley's *That Uncertain Feeling* was getting. Philip's friendship with Kingsley Amis was strong and intimate but tinged with a perhaps inevitable rivalry; he felt that Kingsley always fell on his feet whereas he himself invariably landed on a more central portion of his anatomy. Philip told us, good humouredly, how after reading the manuscript of *That Uncertain Feeling*, he complained that Kingsley had cannibalised his letters for some of the material. 'Life transmuted into art,' Kingsley had retorted. Philip replied, 'But God damn it, Kingsley, my letters ARE art.'

Philip said he had received a letter from Donald Davie complaining about the non-appearance of *Listen*. Philip added that the magazine meant more in the intellectual life of the country than we might have imagined. It was no novelty that the fourth issue of *Listen* was late. Apart from cash-flow problems – we had to pay a large part of one printing bill before we dared run up another – it would have been impossible to do all the work involved in publishing the magazine on a quarterly basis, especially after we launched into book publication and, later, records. We simply did not have the facilities. A few years later, I was amazed and envious to learn that Brian Cox, who sought our advice before starting his *Critical Quarterly*, had among other aids a paid secretary, and this expense was included in his Arts Council grant. What luxury and what a difference subsidy and secretaries would have made to our lives!

It was a lonely and anxious summer for me. While George attended cocktail parties and met T.S. Eliot and lesser London luminaries, I dealt with *Listen* manuscripts, subscriptions, enquiries, bookshop business, kept track of *The Less Deceived* pre-publication sales and devised an adequate book-keeping system. There was constant worry about the arrival of the weekly housekeeping money. But in compensation, the girls and I could live on cheap female food such as eggs, cheese and salads. I was also spared, during this period, the daily slog of turning George out to the high standard his dignity required – no mean feat in those sockdarning, pre-washing-machine days.

When at last the day came for George to return to Hull, he did not want to go; metropolitan life suited him well. Joyce and Steve eagerly packed his case with his clothes and the art objects he had acquired during his stay with them: a Patrick Heron drawing, a large African carving and various books. They knelt on and strapped up the case and saw George off into the train. As he reached the end of the street, Steve said gloomily, 'He's wearing my best braces.'

For a number of years Philip took his annual holiday in Sark. It was quiet, unfashionable and still within the British Isles, which he vowed never to leave. In September 1955 he went there taking *The Less Deceived* proofs with him. He returned the corrected proofs to us saying that he thought five hundred copies was handsome for a first edition. In fact, with last minute optimism we printed seven hundred copies but only bound four hundred. Such was the demand that, in no time at all we had bound up and sold the three hundred sets of sheets and ordered another impression of the book from the printer, only to find that he had, by an oversight, broken up the type. This meant a delay, while the type was re-set, before we could get the book back into print.

We made our sales without benefit of commercial travellers or advertising, apart from exchange columns with other little magazines. Our books, and later our records, sold with the aid of reviews and our readers' recommendations.

In October George returned to work at Austin Reed's Hull shop and the parcels of *The Less Deceived* arrived. All the normal processes of life then ceased until the books had been despatched to subscribers, the press and bookshops. Ones and twos were easily popped into stout manila envelopes but parcels were harder. From Mr Wigby, who let me have groceries on tick, I obtained corrugated card in the form of Omo and Weetabix cartons which I hacked and bent to size. This all proved to be excellent aversion therapy since now, in my fifties, I have a great disinclination to use the postal services and post offices are my least favourite places. We composed letters together and I typed them, working usually very late into the night and then, if the children woke, I had to get up to see to them. Consequently, neither George nor I was much good at getting up in the mornings. Clearly one of us would have to learn to get out of bed if George was to hold down a job. I discovered that sitting bolt upright the moment the alarm rang was fool-proof and since then rising has been no problem.

When the children were older, it was my practice to take George his breakfast on a tray up to bed each morning. I was prompted by low cunning rather than an excess of wifely zeal, since it meant the children and I could have a peaceful meal downstairs. One morning I was busy talking to the gasman, who had come to empty the meter, and I asked Laurien to remove a boiled egg from the pan and take it upstairs to George. With true Scorpio directness she ran upstairs with the egg in a teatowel, bread and butter in the other hand, and shouted, 'Hey! Hold your hands out.' George, half asleep, sat up and did as he was told. She dropped the hot egg into one of his hands, the bread and butter into the other, and retreated smartly. George's cries of pain and outrage followed her down the stairs and she nipped off to school while he was still struggling with his clothes.

Laurien, being the elder of my daughters, always had more clout, but Alison was more devious. Most of the time they got on well together and were very equable – they had to be, since all our lives were subsumed to the needs of The Marvell Press. Ali would suffer under Laurien's tyranny for a while and then decide to get her revenge by cutting Laurien's shoelaces off, an inch a day, until she could no longer tie them.

Meal-times were a trial since there was an edict that everything must be eaten. As Ali was squeamish and virtually a non-eater, Laurien and I were constantly rescuing her from wrath by secreting Ali's rejected fried eggs or kippers about our persons for subsequent disposal. One teatime, going it alone, Ali wrapped three unwanted sausages in her handkerchief, put them up her sleeve and then forgot about them. It was Friday, our cinema night, and they were expected at my mother's. They caught a bus which was full and had to stand up, tightly gripping the leather straps buses used to have. Suddenly Ali felt she was going to sneeze so she pulled her hanky out from the sleeve of her raised arm and the three sausages bounced down the bus ricocheting from one passenger to another. Deeply mortified, Ali decided that Hartley impassivity would be wiser than attempting an explanation. Laurien tried to look as unrelated to her as possible.

George and I were oddities in our social class as was Philip in his. He had none of the brash assurance and general philistinism I associate with the sons of local government officials. Philip's conversation was full of references to the embarrassments life caused him, a host of fears, and the apple cores he had shied that had missed. He had scant confidence that the privileges the rest of his class enjoyed were open to him. We, on the other hand, had refused to accept the cultural standards that our parents had tried to impose on us. There is a cosiness about working-class life which can keep you too safely within the confines of its narrow interests. John Wain, in his novel *Hurry on Down* symbolized this safety and limitation in the phrase 'the brown houses', and Willy Russell brilliantly expands the theme in *Educating Rita*. George and I, determined to sing a different tune, rejected what we were offered.

As the three of us – George, Philip and I – discussed excitedly the latest review or decided what improvements we could make to the next edition of *The Less Deceived,* it often struck me that here was a most unlikely conjunction: Philip, with his conventional and privileged background, and George and I who had not even the gloss of a grammar-school education. Yet we were curiously united by a common interest. My schooling had been interrupted by wartime evacuation, and George's by an almost-fatal bout of rheumatic fever. We had left school at fifteen with no qualifications and no prospects, although we did not feel the lack of a good education at the time since we both had burning ambitions to make some sort of artistic mark.

We were not Leonard and Virginia Woolf and we would probably never be rich, but we felt rather smug as the critical accolades and the bookshop orders flowed in.

Ten

In 1956, still living from hand to mouth but encouraged by the resounding success of *The Less Deceived,* we published not only the fifth issue of *Listen* but also John Holloway's first collection of verse, *The Minute and Longer Poems.* It was a good book and we were delighted that the Poetry Book Society chose it for their members but, having printed too few copies of Philip's book, and thinking that we would save money in the long run, we printed a very large edition of *The Minute.* Also, for this book and all our subsequent publications, we gave the author a percentage royalty on each copy sold, thinking this was a shrewd improvement on the financial arrangement made for *The Less Deceived.* Neither stratagem worked to our benefit in the short and medium run. Although *The Minute* sold well, it sold only steadily, so we were paying royalties for years before we had covered the cost. Since *The Less Deceived* was our first venture and we had nothing to compare it with, it took us some time to realize that the book was an exceptional item in the poetry publishing world – a bestseller. Eventually we acknowledged our beginner's luck and, ignoring the economies of scale (the more you order the cheaper they come) that could leave us with large stocks of unsold books, we began to order smaller editions.

Being a Poetry Book Society choice gave John Holloway's book an excellent start but provided a lot of assembly-line work. The Poetry Book Society subscribers numbered over a thousand at that time, and along came so many sticky labels which had to be licked and stuck on so many parcels, stamped, loaded into the pram and ferried to the village. All this had to be done at publication time when there were review copies to be sent off, with covering letters, to many newspapers and periodicals. The wonderful thing was, of course, that the Poetry Book Society paid on the dot at the end of the month and turned our bank balance from accusing red to acquiescent black.

I seldom met our authors, since none but Philip were local and I could not get far with two young children, but I would hear about them. Philip told me that one of the things which warmed him to John Holloway was that he had a marvellous instinct for the important things in life. Whatever he and Philip might be saying or doing, Holloway would look at his watch and say, 'It's opening time.' It was comments like this and well-oiled evenings at Philip's flat as he carefully prepared drinks and made sure that there were plenty of ice cubes and lemon slices to go with the gin or martini, that made me feel suddenly self-conscious about the dryness of 253 Hull Road. I had come from a home where we had a bottle of port at Christmas, and neither George nor I had ever been solvent enough to develop even a casual drinking habit. One evening, when Philip was coming for a meal, I felt I must provide some alcohol but I only had five shillings left after buying the food so I hiked down to the off-licence with an empty bottle and bought a pint of apricot wine-from-the-wood. I would have done better to buy a few bottles of beer but, like most tramps and novice drinkers, my palate favoured the sweet and sickly. I offered Philip a glass of this stuff. He took a deep swig, then choked, pulled a face, and said, 'Good God, Jean! What's this, Chateau du Dettol?' Years later, seeing his hesitation when I offered him a glass of perfectly respectable dry sherry, I reminded him of this incident. 'Did I really say that? How terribly rude of me.'

I would not recommend publishing on a shoe-string.

Without adequate funds it is difficult to cut any sort of dash at close quarters; we found it much easier to impress and inspire confidence by post. If a literary figure called on us, he or she would discover there was no hall and so visitors had to walk straight into the front room which was a foot lower than the outside path – this gave any caller the initial advantage of towering over the inhabitants. Once inside, we would drink lemon tea, talk about what was new on the poetry scene and, perhaps show our latest publication if we had one hot from the press. Then came the awkward moment when the visitor would ask for the loo and would make for the stairs which rose from the tiny living-room. We would steer him or her out of the back door and past the coalhouse, apologizing on the way for the flooded yard. George made a number of plaster casts from his clay sculptures and the resultant dross had bunged up the drain peculiarly – often the water managed to flow past the blockage but sometimes it did not. We felt no embarrassment with Philip, since he had been a regular visitor from the early days and had accepted all our warts. He would always notice the latest refinement, such as new curtains or wallpaper, and would compliment us on it.

We made occasional faint-hearted attempts at fund raising. There had been some promising correspondence with an elderly millionairess poetaster who lived in Scotland. Since we always took an annual week's holiday in Burnmouth, a small Scottish fishing village where George's mother rented a primitive cottage, we decided one year while we were there to catch a bus to Edinburgh and personally plead our poverty to the lady. Showing us into her exquisite Georgian residence, the butler took my coat and immediately exposed its raggy lining. I wanted to creep away home.

The day was fraught with misunderstanding. The woman's husband kept asking us baffling questions about the climate, the humidity and how long it had taken us to get there. Two large dogs farted gently but persistently

95

under the table throughout lunch. Eventually, overcome by the foul miasma and the surrealistic questions, I said loudly, 'Burnmouth's only sixty miles down the A1', to which he replied, 'Burnmouth? Oh, I thought you said you'd just come from Burma.' Eventually we talked about literature and the problems of publishing. After much thought, the lady gave us a long, judicial look and said, 'What you really need is a little van. That would make all the difference.' Actually, our bus fare back to Hessle would have made all the difference since, for the last few days, the four of us had been maniacally winkling on Burnmouth rocks to try to raise the money. This was my first experience of the gulf between the very rich and the poor.

Still, we had a good lunch and she clearly found George an engaging fellow. On the way out, she murmured to me oracularly, 'You must take care of your beautiful skin, my dear.' The following week she sent us an eight-bob subscription to *Listen* magazine and submitted an enormous batch of her own Yorkshire dialect poems.

Bad debts were a real hardship to us. A bookselling firm owned by Robert Maxwell used to order gratifyingly large quantities of our books, defer payment for some plausible-sounding accounting reason, then order more books. At the end of two years his firm had built up a vast debt (peanuts to them, no doubt) and we were throwing good money after bad by sending them statement after fruitless statement. After threatening them with legal action (which we could not have afforded to take) we received a letter saying they had gone into liquidation. After another long lapse they offered to pay us, through the official receiver, something like eightpence in the pound. Later, such firms would rise like the phoenix in some improved financial form and we would still be struggling to pay our authors and printer.

My own pursuit of poetry had been lonely and Holy Grail-like, a romantic reaching out for the 'silver apples of the moon, the golden apples of the sun.' So I was surprised and disappointed that my daughters, who had the advantage of a house full of books and were on friendly terms with an internationally celebrated poet, should be so apathetic about this form of art. 'Do you really not like poetry?' I asked them. Alison replied that all poetry meant for her was the taste of manila tape. When other kids were out playing, she was licking envelopes and wrapping packages. Poetry for Laurien meant a pramful of parcels wheeled round Hessle on a Sunday and as many as possible stuffed into each postbox until it was full. It is strange that the inhabitants of Hessle did not combine to complain about the crammed post boxes.

We tried to avoid the post office up the road where the surly owners made it clear that they were not best pleased by our cottage industry. 'It's them buggers,' one would whisper to the other as the kids and I unloaded the pram. 'One packet, book post to the Virgin Islands, Singapore and Hong Kong, four to the USA, three to Japan and a hundred eightpenny stamps please. Oh, and there's six different weights of parcels just to go inland.' I would try to sound authoritative and confident but I would be guiltily aware that a dozen assorted pension and family allowance customers were sighing behind me.

Officials were remarkably tolerant. Once when some difficulty arose over an unreturned manuscript, the local constabulary sent their most literary policeman to sort it out. After the formalities were over, he sat down, took off his helmet and asked us about possible outlets for the short stories he wrote.

During the years when George was unemployed – the Austin Reed job was short-lived – although we made no profit and therefore had no reason to feel guilt, we lived behind masks. Opening the front door to callers was always prefaced by discreet net-curtain twitching. If the caller was the milkman, we hid under the table as he was likely to go round the back for his money and would spot us. Unidentifiable visitors elicited a blank-faced response until we knew whether to adopt our Marvell Press do-come-in-and-take-out-a-subscription-to-*Listen* face or our poverty pleading look-we've-got-no-carpets face for the man from the National Assistance Board.

We aimed to publish at least one book a year and four issues of *Listen*. But as I said, we did not accomplish this aim as far as *Listen* was concerned. In 1957, only two numbers came out – one cover designed by George and the other by Stanley Chapman. Stanley, our good and faithful designer, would always oblige us with something fresh and original but, modestly, to avoid seeing his name in print yet again, he would sign the drawings 'Quatrezo-neilles' or 'Marie-Louise Chenapan'. Since *The Less Deceived,* Philip had let us have his poems 'Tops', 'Days', 'Water', and 'Referred Back' for different issues of *Listen* and, in Vol. 2 No. 3, we printed his splendid piece of 're-quired writing', 'The Pleasure Principle': putatively a review of three books, the first four paragraphs constitute his own poetic credo. The piece is as coherent and un-selfconscious as the rest of his writing. He puts the subject of the demand for poetry in the prosaic terms one might think more appropriate to well-served food or good-quality cloth, and he defines the complex process that goes into the creation and communication of a poem as 'de-livering the goods'. More often than not (to use a Larkin-like qualification) and more regularly than most twentieth-century poets, despite his modest output, he de-livered the goods and they seldom failed to please.

But we kept up our schedule on the book publication front with *Home Truths,* a first collection by Anthony Thwaite, who had recently returned from Japan. It re-ceived the excellent reviews we had come to expect of the work of our poets: '. . . here complex adult experience is forged into works of art. It is a real achievement that, for once, "impressive" really is the right word.' – *The Specta-tor.* We printed our usual list of subscribers at the end of the book but, though it sold well, we had again made the mistake of over-producing and therefore it took us a long time to break even.

We lived an extremely busy life, keeping so many balls in the air, and my time was filled with the minutiae of running the press smoothly, as well as the home, so we saw few people and we really looked forward to Philip's visits.

Most weeks Philip would have a good moan about the aridity of his sex life and would perhaps mention, enviously, how he had seen so-and-so (a university colleague) coming out of a tutorial room with his arm around some toothsome undergraduate. 'He's no doubt having it off with her. Lucky sod.' But I think he was too polite, diffident and 'gentlemanly' to have the sort of rakish success he thought he wanted, and also, I imagine, too fastidious. A typical complaint would start thus: 'Sex is so difficult. You ought to be able to get it and pay for it monthly like the laundry bill. I'm pissed off with the effort that has to be put in for so little return. You meet a girl and she seems to fancy you so you invite her round to your flat. The lights are low and you've spent pots of money on caviar and poured expensive champagne into her. Then, just as you're about to move in for the big seduction scene, she starts talking about this bloke she's engaged to.' To the determined lecher this would merely add more relish and glory to the ultimate success whereas to Philip it spelled retirement and defeat.

Publication of *The Less Deceived* brought Philip lots of fan letters. It took me some time to internalize the fact that a portion of our morning post might be for him. I remember, after sleepily opening three of his on successive days and then apologetically forwarding them, feeling wounded when I received a very curt note from him in which he suggested I should find myself some reading material other than his private letters. Still, it had the desired effect and subsequently I remembered to put on my specs and separate the letters into two piles before opening any of them. One letter he received stirred and disturbed him. A woman had written to ask him to meet her in the basement of Hammond's department store. He spent a great deal of time deliberating about this but ruefully decided that 'You can't, can you?' I would have gone like a shot – and no doubt lived to regret it. He also received letters from budding poets who were anxious to solicit his opinion of their work. He was always kind to people who sent him poems and he had a stock reply that included a phrase about it being 'a triumph for you to have finished this'.

One day he brought round to tea a large, pretty woman who knitted all evening except when eating. From an upper-clergy background, she had recently worked in a factory for the fun of it. Some fun thought I, who had narrowly escaped that working life as my fate. She told us she bought *The Daily Mirror* every day in order to be like the rest. Next time we saw Philip I remarked on her charms. He said, reflectively, 'I think she'd like to marry me. At least she'd have her own money.' This last point seemed very important to him. On the subject of choosing a life-partner, Philip always maintained that it was safest to marry the boy or girl next door. This was usually accompanied by a meaningfully approving look at me and George which displayed a more sanguine view of our marriage than the truth warranted. It would never do to marry a foreigner he said, shuddering with horror. Nuances of expression subtly altered meaning and made it difficult enough to understand the minds and hearts of those whose language and background you shared. God knows what problems you might have with someone from abroad: the scope for misunderstanding would be endless.

Eleven

When we heard Philip's poems read in refined Third Programme tones, the readings often seemed to alter emphasis and therefore the meaning that Philip had intended. Sometimes the voice would rise when we knew it should fall. We felt strongly that the poet's own reading must be the definitive one and so we started our own label, Listen Records, inaugurating it with a recording of Philip reading *The Less Deceived*. Though it is sad that Philip's poetic *oeuvre* was not larger, one of the virtues of his slim volumes is that each fits comfortably on to a long-playing record.

Philip was never an enthusiastic public reader of his own verse. In 1956 we had toyed with the idea of issuing a recorded anthology of a selection of our *Listen* poets reading their own work. The venture proved to be unwieldy and we eventually dropped it. Naturally we invited Philip to contribute, without much hope of getting him to agree. Indeed his response was unequivocally negative. He was worried; no one had ever asked him to record anything before, and if they had he would have declined. He insisted he had vowed never to read in public as he would be no good at it. By the middle of 1958, however, we had managed to coax him to change his mind with the prospect of a lush sleeve and the excitement of photographic expeditions to the Spring Bank Cemetery. ('Do me blurred and in the distance.') The Cemetery would have some link with 'Church Going', one of the book's strongest and most celebrated poems.

The Spring Bank Cemetery was one of Philip's favourite haunts. Opened in 1847, it did away with the disgraceful intra-mural burials that had taken place in overflowing church graveyards and it accommodated the ever-increasing number of cholera victims. Originally situated on the outskirts of town, by the 1950s it had become a large area of rampant inner city dereliction, its eastern end unfenced and spilling out on to the surrounding pavements. Once inside the wilderness, one was soon knee-high in couch grass, elder, bramble and the tangled ivy that climbed up the overhanging trees. Creepers twined romantically round leaning angels and rioted over fat cherubs. Black Magic ceremonies were reputed to take place there at dead of night but in the daytime it provided a sculpturally rich, light-dappled refuge for those of a contemplative nature. What had once been order and regimentation had now returned to wild woodland and been reclaimed by the fox. Manpower Services schemes have since tamed and fenced the area, setting the tombstones straight and hacking away the dark undergrowth. But in 1958 the cemetery was still a glorious jungle and a perfect visual metaphor for that element in Philip's make-up which rejoiced in the anarchic and – even for someone as guiltily ambivalent about money as he – the untidy and uncommercial.

In a letter to a local councillor dated 11 October 1977, Philip made an eloquent plea for the preservation of the cemetery's unique character and, to that end, he gave details of the work he felt should be done. He described the place as 'a natural cathedral, an inimitable blended growth of nature and humanity of over a century, something that no other town could create whatever its resources.' In 1964, during the filming of the BBC's Monitor programme, Philip had taken John Betjeman to see 'the most beautiful spot in Hull'. By chance, the local Hull artist, W. A. Sillince (well known for his cartoons which appeared in *Punch*), who knew Betjeman slightly, happened to be working there. Sillince made lots of lightning sketches from which he subsequently produced a number of water-colour paintings, one of which he called 'Betjeman's Oak'. Philip bought the picture and sent it to Betjeman.

Once the photographs for the sleeve were developed, we spent enjoyable hours pouring over books of display type. When we asked Philip whether he would like the cover photo to have a border or a bleed-off, his face lit up. 'Bleed-off. What a satisfying phrase! Christ, the number of people I'd like to have said that to this week – "Oh, bleed-off you fucker".' Meeting Philip reconciled me to my own unrestrained swearing habit. I excused it to myself on the grounds that, with a working-class background, it was a disease you could not help catching but, at the same time, I could not help feeling that it was the last resort of the in-articulate. Hearing some of Philip's well-constructed curses, however, made me appreciate swearing as an art form.

Philip emphasised to us that the sleeve note he wrote for the record was not an attempt to sing the praises of The Marvell Press but rather to present the historical facts of the book's publication. He regarded the story as quite a romantic one and, here and there, rather funny. He wished to retain copyright of the piece but allowed us to appear to have copyright to avoid declaring his authorship.

Determined to have the best, Philip and George went off to HMV studios where we imagined we would get a perfect recording but there was, in fact, some noise. Philip felt that the 'poltergeist background' was distracting but claimed that a visitor to whom he played it had noticed nothing untoward. He reported that the first time he played the record, the needle jumped twice on the first track. I can imagine Philip thinking that the sod's law which he felt presided over most Larkin enterprises was once again in operation, but fortunately the jumps did not occur on subsequent playings.

He thought that his reading sounded amateurish and

that much of it was toneless ('I think the sleeve is the best part about it'), but was pleased that he had been able to read most of it without hesitation. He described this as 'a little miracle'. There are just one or two places where Philip makes a sort of clenched-palate-tongue-sucking sound, a bit like a bushman click, which was the strategy he used to overcome his stammer.

The record was a financial success and the project not too risky since the economics of record production are such that you can press a hundred at a time, according to demand and what you can afford, whereas with books you need initially to print a large number in order to cover the enormous cost of typesetting (each successive hundred comes a bit cheaper). The reviews were mixed. One reviewer described Philip's voice as being 'colourless as tapwater': I have always found it attractive and expressive. Fortunately fashions change. Who would now prefer anyone else's interpretations of Larkin poems to Philip's? His witty sleeve note for the record's second cover is a delightful and as yet uncollected piece of writing. Here is an excerpt from it:

Interviewer: Were you used to reading your poems when you made this record?
Larkin: As a matter of fact I'd done it only once, for the British Council. They shut you up alone in a room with a live microphone and tell you to read, talk, anything you like. One man went to sleep. But this record was made in a very busy and rather noisy commercial studio; it was probably all right for making a private record for your New Zealand cousins of your daughter singing 'Over the Rainbow', but with a quiet thing like the speaking voice there were all sorts of extra noises that were upsetting – people going upstairs, and pulling lavatory chains and so on.

In 1959, we published one issue of *Listen, The Less*

Deceived record, and Donald Davie's collection of poems *The Forests of Lithuania*. This is a long, richly descriptive narrative poem which Davie adapted from the classic *Pan Tadeusz* by the Polish writer Adam Mickiewicz. The book was attractively produced with a Bewick wood-cut on the dust jacket and a frontispiece, of a Lithuanian bison, drawn by Howard Warshaw. It was a financially successful venture for, this time, we erred on the cautious side and published quite a small edition which quickly sold out – though the edition was not small by average poetry book standards since we had a hundred and eight pre-publication subscribers and, like the Holloway book, it was chosen by the Poetry Book Society. This gave us an initial sale of over a thousand copies. After the book went out of print, we regretted not having ordered the printing of a few hundred more copies. But that is the art of publishing: knowing just how many the market will take.

Listen magazine not only printed a good cross-section of poetry but it also provided a showcase for critics such as Donald Davie, L. D. Lerner, Charles Madge, Malcolm Bradbury, Arthur Terry, Frank Kermode, Alan Brownjohn and Allan Rodway. *Listen* record sleeves also furnished space for essays to be printed, such as Kingsley Amis's explanation, on the back of the *Case of Samples* L.P., of his reasons for writing poetry. We reprinted, from the *New Statesman,* Philip Larkin's sensitive appraisal of Stevie Smith's poems on the back of her *Selected Poems* L.P., and Christopher Ricks' fine evaluation of Philip Larkin's poetry appeared on the reverse of the *Whitsun Weddings* L.P.

We thought of publishing a novel. No one gets rich by publishing poetry; since poetry readers are in a minority, you are lucky to break even. Most big publishers publish poetry for prestige, and only the exceptionally popular poet, such as John Betjeman, makes much in the way of profit for them. John Barth's novel *The End of the Road* was one we toyed with the idea of publishing. Also Donleavy's

The Ginger Man which had been published in Paris by Maurice Girodias of the Olympia Press in a pornographic series that included such titles as *Whip Angels* and *White Thighs*. It had a limited circulation. But the cost of type-setting a novel would have been so much higher than setting a book of poems that we would have needed to sell a greater number to break even. Meanwhile that huge printer's bill would be on the doormat even before the reviews were out. Our one piece of financial luck was getting £600 from the Gulbenkian Foundation to buy recording equipment, though this was to come later.

Listen always ran at a loss but for a while the deficit was covered for us by the Arts Council under the kindly auspices of Eric Walter White. Having your losses covered is fine but it does not help you to expand. Always the lack of capital stopped us growing any larger or becoming more efficient. Over the years, our standard of living did improve – but it could hardly have got worse.

Much pioneering DIY was attempted at 253 but it mostly back-fired and left us in a more primitive state than before. Whenever George and his father (a spry little man who looked like a cloth-capped Valentino) set to work with hammers and nails, the reciprocal curses would fly: 'You bloody old fool! That was my foot.' 'Well, you should have got it out the road, you daft get!'

One afternoon George and I went out and left his father upstairs trying to transform the minuscule boxroom, which had no floor, into a bathroom. I came back a couple of hours later and, finding the house empty, pottered about the kitchen preparing a meal. I am not very observant, even of things that are at eye-level, so it was a good half hour before I looked up and noticed a great father-in-law-shaped hole in the kitchen ceiling. It was alarming but, since there was no corpse to be seen, I deduced that he had managed to drag himself home. He came back in the evening looking no worse for wear and, when I asked what had happened, he answered laconically, 'Woodworm in the bastard joists.'

One of the minor blights to marital harmony was the back garden – a long, narrow strip of grass intersected by a public footpath, mercifully only used by the dustmen and Trev, Doris, Sandra and Brian Deasle who lived next door. Fortunately, few people realized it was a right of way for it was alarming enough, when munching breakfast, suddenly to see through the window Trev Deasle's dour visage, a few feet away, without the whole of Hull Road, Hessle marching through our garden.

We had no garden tools and in the summer, when the girls were old enough, George would send them out to cut the knee-high grass with scissors and breadknife. I did the best I could to tame it but the lumpy bit at the end of the garden defeated me. For years I nagged George to go out and dig it but he stood fast, and eventually I reconciled myself to this. So it was a surprise and delight when, one sunny summer afternoon, George announced that he thought he would do some gardening. I could not get him outside fast enough and, pointing out to him our only tool, a spade, I retired indoors to do some Marvell Press work. Friday was our only weekly night out and we would regularly leave the children with my mother while we went to the pictures. This was a Friday so I was keen to get the orders and accounts out of the way.

After half an hour, I thought I would go outside to encourage the worker. When I opened the back door, I saw what appeared to be a war victim, covered in blood, dragging his way towards me through the grass. My first thought was of sticking plaster, but when I examined the ghastly cut on George's forehead and saw that the flesh was cloven to the bone I knew it was an ambulance job. While we were waiting for the ambulance to arrive, I said, 'I suppose we won't be able to see the James Dean film after all then?' 'You insensitive bitch!' he groaned through teeth as well gritted as he could manage, considering he had just knocked loose a top front one.

Conditioned as they were to the bizarre goings-on at

107

253, the neighbours had come to rely on us for light entertainment and they formed a guard of honour as George was pushed to the ambulance in a wheelchair. He explained to the attendants that he had lifted his spade to heave it down mightily on a clod of earth but it had hit the clothes-line and rebounded back, knocking him unconscious. The Indian doctor on the ward looked at his notes and his wound and asked, 'What is the name of this weapon you were using?' 'A spade,' George replied, and for the two days that he stayed there he became known as 'the gardener'. Needless to say, it was all my fault for leaving the clothes-line up, and it was George's last foray into horticulture.

Twelve

My father died in 1960. Harry had learnt from my mother's letters to him in New Zealand that my father's health was deteriorating so, after three exciting years down under, he took the long boat journey back. When Dad left the army, C. D. Holmes had given him a relatively light job of crane driving. The work was easier than labouring in the foundry, but all the fumes, dust and noxious particles rose to crane level. The extraction equipment was the lungs of the men who worked there.

For the last few months before Dad died, he was at home 'on sick'. He was not used to idleness and took it hard; he helped my mother with the household chores but it was not his idea of what a man should do. He liked to be out and earning a living. My father slipped away, uncomplainingly, one foggy morning in February. His last words to me the night before, as he struggled for each breath, were: 'Tell me the truth. Am I really dying?' I did not go to see him in the chapel of rest. I wanted to remember him as he used to be when, early in the mornings, I would come down to find him eating his breakfast, wearing his work gear – old trousers, flannelette shirt and a waistcoat, with a big red and white cotton hanky tied gypsy fashion round his neck. He would offer me his pint mug of tea, a good navvy's brew laced with condensed milk and plenty of sugar, from which he and I took alternate gulps. I remember too the evenings when, after I had washed my hair, he would ask me for the hairbrush and while I sat on the floor leaning against his knees, he would patiently brush my hair until it was dry and crackled with electricity.

For years afterwards I would see him in the distance, just turning a corner, and I would run to catch up with him and then slacken pace remembering that he was dead. Or I would see him walking towards me dressed in his best – grey trilby and dark overcoat – and my heart would miss a beat. When he drew level with me I would be moved by the similarity of the man to my father: a bright-eyed, hollow-cheeked working man, worn to the bone but still upright.

In 1960 George went back to study at the local Art College (where he met Ted Tarling who, in 1970, was to start his own magazine, *Wave,* under the imprint of The Sonus Press) but he received no grant, so I got a full-time job with a Hull firm of chartered accountants.

Laurien was nine and Alison seven when I started working again. It was a great wrench, from what had been an informal island of domestic and publishing activity, to a 41-hour week in an office where there were all kinds of tacit conventions to be kept. I have always been the world's worst typist whose best friend was the eraser (thank God for correction fluid). My shorthand was almost forgotten – it had never been more than rudimentary. What recommended me to employers was my 'refined' voice (regional accents were not fashionable at that time and aspirers to middle-class culture laundered their speech accordingly), the fact that I could spell and punctuate, and the spurious look of efficiency that spectacles often lend.

I borrowed some money from my mother to buy some pencil-slim office clothes and a pair of high-heeled shoes. These were *de rigueur* in 1960 – though I agree with the feminist writer who maintains that high heels slow down the brain. I clip-clopped to the bus stop, every morning,

110

accompanied by the children who 'set me off' before they went to school. I hated stockings and did not wear them until the general air of disapproval, expressed in coughs, tut-tuts, sighs and you-must-be-very-cold, Jean, pushed me into conforming. With them went the dreaded 'light-control foundation garment' to keep the bloody stockings up. On hot summer days, or centrally-heated winter ones, the air in the office would be redolent of burning rubber. I learnt to keep very quiet about the publishing business, which my colleagues considered a queer hobby, and I parried questions about our way of life after realizing that frankness would involve a long list of shameful admissions: 'What! You mean to say that you have a typewriter but you haven't got a television/fridge/bathroom/indoor loo/dressing-table/three piece suite . . . ? The catalogue of the requisites of decency was endless. My ignorance of the doings and the exact composition of the Royal Family also earned me black marks.

On the other hand the office was an improvement on the cloister that 253 represented. I was earning £585 per annum which was enough to keep us, at a fairly low level, and the social intercourse, although limited to office hours and not stimulating in the same way as George's art college course, made me feel younger and more confident.

I met few of the writers we corresponded with, but George was now beginning to meet people who lived locally, knew of my existence and therefore included me in their invitations. When Malcolm Bradbury worked at Hull University, he and his wife Elizabeth bought a cottage at Lockington – a quiet and remote village although it was only ten miles or so from Hull. Cleverly furnished and adorned with saleroom bargains, their cottage looked quaint, homely and exuded culture. Weekends spent in their hospitable household made a welcome break for me after time spent filling in pig-farmers' income-tax returns at work and carrying out the Marvell Press routine at home. They had all the latest books and records and I loved the atmosphere of happiness and industry they had both created. A typical visit would start with a meal, talk of books and literary personalities – we listened avidly to their reports of meeting such stars as Saul Bellow and Robert Lowell – and then they might play us their new L.P. of Tom Lehrer or their musical version of *Candide*. The cottage was filled with evidence of their literary activity and I remember, after one visit, saying in amazement: 'George, did you notice that they've even got a typewriter in the lavatory?' That was real artistic dedication.

Being in company removed the temptation to behave badly. Back at home there was always scope for a row. Its sequel generally took the form of me packing a suitcase and marching off, accompanied by the kids, in the direction of Hessle foreshore. There we would fulminate against George, discuss ways and means, decide there weren't any, and return a few hours later when the temperature inside 253 had dropped somewhat.

On one occasion we were almost at the village when the unmistakable Scottish tones of George's mother's voice could be heard hailing us from a distance. When she caught up with us it was to ask us to return immediately as 'two poetry fellers' had turned up and needed to be entertained. Keeping up a good front for outsiders was something we had always endeavoured to do and only the trained observer ever perceived signs of strife. (Laurien once said, 'I knew you'd had a row when I saw the macedoine on the wall.') Hiding the suitcase in the garden, we strolled in as if from a shopping expedition, and greeted Anthony Thwaite. He had brought with him Mark Bonham-Carter who was, at that time, making a documentary film in the north of England. Tea and friendly chit-chat followed and I was impressed when Mark B.-C., asking for the loo, automatically made for the backyard. I was less impressed, however, when on his return, he swooped to admire a Bonnard *Nude in the Bath* print that I had framed. 'Where did you get this?' he asked, implying that it must be the original. I shamefacedly admitted having cut it out of the *Sunday Times* colour section. My embarrassment was quite irrational and I suppose the mistake was natural enough since we had, by then, acquired some choice drawings: a Patrick Heron nude, some Henry Moore sketches and a small Burne-Jones that George had picked up in London.

Since our days were fully occupied, the publishing activities had to be squeezed into evenings and weekends. We were so busy despatching records, books and magazines that the appearance of *Listen* had become even more erratic than usual. To make up for a long gap, we published a double number, Volume 3 Numbers 3 and 4, which contained reviews and a good selection of American verse along with some poems by English writers. Among them was one of my favourites, Philip's 'Before Tea' which he retitled 'Afternoons' when he included it in *Whitsun Weddings*. I love the economical way he captures the prosaic nature of the women's lives yet links, so lyrically, the natural image of summer fading with the ageing of the young women. The phrase 'their beauty has thickened' most aptly describes what happens to people and trees. I find this one of his most haunting poems on the defacing effects of time.

We charged four shillings for the double number. Looking now at the Kraus Reprint edition, 1969, which collected all twelve issues of *Listen* into one bound volume, I can only marvel that, despite inflation, we kept the price of a normal issue down to two shillings.

We were lucky that our contributors settled for gratitude rather than money. We sent each of them two complimentary copies of the magazine. I suppose the distinction of appearing in a much-praised periodical which maintained its high standards was sufficient to keep them submitting their manuscripts. I also think we were all less materialistic in those days. The purchase of one issue, Volume 3 Number 2 for example, would give you a cover designed by Henry Moore (he did three of our covers), a new canto by Ezra Pound, poems by Byron Colt, Thom Gunn, Elizabeth Jennings, Richard Murphy, D.J. Enright, Alan Neame, Margaret Owen, Fergus Allen, and criticism by Philip Larkin, Allan Rodway and Arthur Terry.

John Sankey, our amiable printer, came up to see us from time to time, roaring up from London in his superb Aston Martin. Parked outside the house, it added a great deal to our standing with the neighbours and I insisted on being photographed draped over the bonnet. John would come bearing a chicken and a bottle of wine which made a welcome change from the risotto we had been eating for weeks. 'Too much ris and not enough otto,' was Alison's verdict on one batch.

George was never short of a grand scheme or two. One year he dreamed up the idea of a huge charity concert, 'Pop for Oxfam' (twenty odd years in advance of Bob Geldof). George was the director and Ted Tarling (on the understanding that he would not be required to listen to a note of the stuff), Harry Duffin, another art-student friend, and I constituted the committee. Although we were all jazz fans, we could see that a big pop festival held in Wembley Stadium could raise a vast sum of money for charity and would be an exciting event to organize. A letterhead was printed and a host of notable people agreed to sponsor us to the extent of letting us use their names; they ranged from Henry Moore to Brian Epstein – Benjaman Britten turned us down but wished us luck. Armed with this support and full of hope, George went to Oxfam's headquarters to outline the scheme. At first they accepted it but later turned it down on the grounds that one of our sponsors was (unknown to us) a manufacturer of armaments. We had not done our homework well enough.

Thirteen

One of Oliver Mackrill's audit clerks lived in Bridlington. He told me Louis Armstrong was to play a one-night stand there at the Spa. I asked him to get me four tickets and I invited Philip, who was overjoyed at the prospect of seeing one of his idols in the flesh. How would we get there? Few but the rich had cars in those days. Our pretty, young, art-student friend, Janet Snowden, came to call on us while we trying to resolve this problem and she thought she might be able to borrow her mother's ancient vehicle.

After the war the British Musician's Union made a rule prohibiting American bands from coming over here to play to the general public, although they were allowed to perform for their troops at military bases. As is usual after wars, unemployment was widespread, and the Union aimed to keep whatever jobs there were for British musicians. During the late 1950s, under the auspices of Norman Grantz, the jazz impresario, exchanges began and, though I do not wish to disparage the British artists, we certainly seemed to get the best of the deal. During the 1960s there was a feast of concerts in civic halls throughout the country. Shoe-horned into the back of a friend's minivan, George and I made evening pilgrimages to Leeds, Sheffield and Manchester to hear Ella Fitzgerald, Duke Ellington, Count Basie, Coleman Hawkins, Sonny Stitt and a score of other legendary musicians.

On one of these occasions, Keith Smith had offered to pick up George outside the Art College on his way home from work at 5.30 p.m. A grey mini-van, stopped by the traffic lights, appeared there at the appointed time and George climbed into the passenger seat. Always embarrassed, silent and awkward in the initial stages of any encounter, George sat bolt upright staring ahead as the driver negotiated the difficult rush-hour traffic. Gradually George became aware that the van's dashboard and cubbyholes did not contain the usual Smith impedimenta. Finally, he cast a covert glance at the driver which established that he was, in fact, a total stranger. Too gobsmacked to comment, the driver watched George get out at the next set of traffic lights and prepare to walk back to the college, no words having been exchanged by either party.

The Spa Royal Hall, on the Bridlington seafront, was a most unlikely venue for Armstrong and Co., with its lofty glass-domed rotunda and 1930s basket chairs ranged round the pastel tinted walls. The ambience would have been more suited to a variety show and, indeed, the audience seemed to be composed of whole families from grandads to granddaughters. We sat impatiently through the supporting band's efforts – it was a well-meaning sextet, wearing striped blazers and straw boaters, who lacked volume and made little impression in the vast and echoing hall which had been designed for twenty-piece bands.

'Look! They've even got potted palms', said Janet during the interval. She was impressed when Philip, in true student fashion, took a book from his pocket and started making notes – for his diary presumably. We feared that Armstrong would be inaudible but the first notes he blew, as the group walked on, assured us that their decibel level was entirely adequate. We were seeing a great trumpeter, past his prime, rather stagily using his handkerchief to mop his brow and, understandably, not busting a gut for his hick audience. Nevertheless, I was moved to tears a couple of times: once during 'Blueberry Hill' and again when he sang a superb, slow-tempo version of 'A Kiss to Build a Dream on'. It was a memorable evening, not least because it took us several hours to do the thirty-mile journey home. Janet's mother's car was an elderly Vauxhall and on the way back the clutch kept slipping. Was it contentment at having 'seen Louis plain', or despair at never seeing his bed that night, that kept Philip slumped in his seat as we drove, very slowly, back to Hull? I seem to remember that he repaid our treat by taking us to see a performance of *The Seagull* at the University.

We had acquired a second-hand piano which, when he felt like it, Philip would sit at to tinkle out a blues. As soon as I watched him, or complimented him on his playing, he would stop and say, 'No, I can't really play.' At that time Miles Davis's 'Kind of Blue' was rarely off our turntable. Philip listened politely to whatever we played and, eventually admitted to liking Davis, but in general our taste was too modern for him.

Some years later, Philip bought a car. Seeing his car in the University car park, and knowing his antipathy to the music of Charlie Parker, my friend, Frank Redpath, put a note under his windscreen which read, 'Tremble Larkin: Bird Lives'. Eventually Frank owned up to the practical joke and Philip expressed relief at the clearing up of this small but nagging enigma.

Philip would try out on us phrases he was polishing for his *Daily Telegraph* reviews, such as the delightful, 'Miles Davis and Ornette Colman stand in evolutionary relationship to each other like green apples and stomach-ache.' George was keen on Coltrane, Parker, Colman, Monk and Gillespie. I could take or leave Colman, especially at the ear-shattering volume George insisted on playing him but I still enjoy the other musicians when I hear them. I lost the record collection (and almost everything else) by divorce and have never got round to replacing it.

Philip was a great enthusiast and encourager. When I mentioned that I was trying to find a recording of 'Tishomingo Blues', he brought me a copy the next week, and I shall always be grateful to him for introducing me to Billie Holliday's music.

He often recommended authors to me – Christina Rossetti, Henry de Montherlant, Flann O'Brien, Barbara Pym, Peter de Vries for example – and he actually lent me some books but he always recorded the loan in a little book, with name and date alongside. I wish I had adopted this practice. Many of my favourite books have been pressed on people I have wanted to share them with and have never been returned.

Once Philip had decided to lend you a book he would go straight to the appropriate shelf and pick it out immediately – so unlike my frantic searches from room to room or the temporising, 'I know I've got it *somewhere* because I used it to press some flowers, weigh down the paté, etc.' As he handed the volume over, he would drop his chin and give you the over-the-top-of-the-specs, librarian stare that dared you not to return it within the fortnight. It was the look I got when I was six years old and stood at the counter of the Boulevard Branch Library saying, 'Please can I join?' 'Let me see your hands.' came the suspicious reply, and they were duly inspected, back and front, for cleanliness.

One year when Philip and Maeve Brennan, his colleague and friend, came to pay us their usual Christmas visit, Philip had brought my daughters a doll each. At the opening of the Philip Larkin Memorial Exhibition at the Brynmor Jones Library, 2 June 1986, Maeve reminded me of the occasion and of her astonishment at seeing Philip hand over the dolls; it seemed an unlikely purchase for him to make. He was careful with money. I am sure he did not need to be since he had always earned well, lived small, and saved. Yet, money, or the lack of it, was something he always felt insecure and frightened about.

There were many satisfactions in Philip's life at this time. His library job and his writing activities had proved to be compatible.

His attitude to his book being stocked by local bookshops had completely changed: 'I was in Brown's today and they only had two copies of *The Less Deceived* left. Do make sure they always have a dozen.' Also the new library building was now complete and ready to be officially opened. Philip arrived one day in June 1960, looking unusually buoyant. He told us about his meeting with the Queen Mother and described how he had shaved twice that morning yet, by lunch time, he still seemed to have 'convict's chin'. He mimicked beautifully the Vice Chancellor's lilting Welsh accent, 'This is Mr Larkin our poet-librarian,' and the Queen Mother's piping reply, 'Oh, what a lovely thing to be.'

For a number of years Philip wanted me to work for him as his secretary but the pay would have been too poor to keep a family of four – even worse than I was getting at Oliver Mackrill. The lengthy journey to and from the University would have involved taking two buses, and I felt some reservation about working for a man all week and being his publisher at weekends. Although I would have had the chance to deepen my friendship with him, there was a pernickety side to Philip, which surfaced from time to time in our business dealings, and I would have found that difficult to accept. Also, I see now that, if I had taken the job, I would have remained a shorthand-typist, whereas my lecturing job, in which I discussed poetry and encouraged students to read it, gave me more satisfaction – and financial reward – than I ever received from office work.

Our most interesting book, from the publishing point of view, was our reprint in 1960 of Ezra Pound's 1916 memoir, *Gaudier-Brzeska*. Pound was keen to see this in print again with better illustrations and some additions to the text. The standard work on this gifted and tragic artist is H. S. Ede's *Savage Messiah,* also out of print at that time. Reading this well-documented and poignant book made us very keen to bring Brzeska's work to a wider audience. Doing so produced much lively correspondence with Pound, H.S.Ede, Pound's daughter, the Musée d'Orleans, and numerous bodies who might have blocks and photographs to lend us. Our problem, as usual, was lack of cash; only the promise of a sale of an edition to an American publisher, New Directions, made the venture financially possible. If the book was to be republished it ought to be well illustrated. We could afford to have only a limited number of new blocks made so we had to borrow the rest. Pound's closely typed airletters to us were marvels of despatch and didacticism: 'Get clichés from Schloss Brunnenberg: EMBRACERS, HIERATIC HEAD, et al. Boris (Pound's son-in-law) will do leg work. Read Peter Goullart's *Forgotten Kingdom*. Write to Basil Bunting. A booklist would follow, drawn from a wide assortment of cultures and languages, along with Pound's comments on what was to be gained from reading them. Each letter could have been printed as a Canto.

I thought Ken Russell made a splendid cinematic version of *Savage Messiah*. The lives of Gaudier and Sophie could so easily have been sensationalised but he resisted this and turned out a film that is restrained, funny and moving.

By now our house was bursting with books and records. There were no cupboards at 253 and the rooms were tiny. Most of our bookstock and wrapping materials were stacked against the walls of the two bedrooms and each new publishing departure took up a little more living space. At about the time when we started the *Listen* record imprint, we bought a handsome garden shed in which to keep the stock. It got a bit spidery over the years but it freed the bedrooms and we no longer stubbed our toes when groping back to bed.

Without some storage, we would have been hard pressed. By now we had published another collection of poems, *Heart's Needle,* by the American poet W. D. Snodgrass, and L.P.'s by Robert Graves, Kingsley Amis and Thom Gunn. We had also pioneered the long-playing 33⅓, seven-inch gramophone record. It accompanied a most elegant looking production of a set of poems by

Donald Davie about the French settlement of North America. Donald signed a limited edition of 350 for us and these copies sold at five shillings more than the unsigned ones. Ted Tarling gave me an account of the recording session:

In November 1961, George and I travelled down to Linton (a village twelve miles north of Cambridge) to stay with Barbara [Ted's sister] for a few days. The purpose of our visit was to record Donald Davie, at Caius College, reading *A Sequence for Francis Parkman*. The recording would be published as part of the first of an intended series of Listenbooks – a Listenbook was to be a volume of poetry which would include, in a sleeve at the back of the book, a gramophone record of the poet reading the poems.

The morning after we arrived, George telephoned Donald to tell him we were on our way to meet him in his room at Caius early in the afternoon.

We missed the bus, walked about ten miles, were given a lift by a frail old lady in a frail old motor car and, partly because of her misdirection, spent ages finding the College. We found it and an anxious Donald Davie in the late afternoon.

Over a glass of sherry, we enjoyed a brief look at what little could be seen of the court from his room, and Donald produced a tape-recorder which he had borrowed from someone who was no longer there to tell us how to make it work. We couldn't even discover how to open the lid of the thing, if there was a lid, or see any sign of a socket where a lead might join it. And where was the lead? We poked and prodded this large, grey, plastic egg as vigorously as we dared, bearing in mind it didn't belong to us, until, as darkness fell, we were reduced to staring at it willing it to hatch and reveal its secret. It didn't.

While George and I discussed this setback, Donald

telephoned his wife to tell her we'd be late for dinner. I said my sister owned a tape-recorder and it was agreed we should travel to Linton, in Donald's motor car, to make the recording.

We arrived at Linton to discover Barbara had left to visit a theatre in Cambridge. I remembered she had lent her tape-recorder to a neighbour. The neighbour, it transpired, had accompanied her to the theatre.

On the way back to Cambridge, Donald wondered whether a writer friend, Douglas Brown, might be at home. Donald spoke warmly of him and was obviously in awe of his academic prowess. Clearly, we were about to meet a man who could take tape-recorders in his stride. This time we were lucky. And he owned a tape-recorder.

While Donald spoke to his wife on the telephone, Douglas Brown explained to George his machine's idiosyncrasies and George asked if he had some spare recording tape he might use. An old spool of tape which contained music Douglas Brown didn't wish to preserve was found and, at last, the recording session began.

I sat very still for half an hour while Donald read his poems and George, uncertainly and almost continuously, fiddled with the controls. When the recording was played back, our faces fell: Douglas Brown's unregarded music could be heard throughout, *con sordino*, accompanying Donald's voice. George said the whole thing would have to be erased before a second attempt could be made. This would take half an hour, of course.

Eventually, after several frustrated attempts, during which Donald read faultlessly, a successful recording was made – though even this was slightly marred, during the reading of *A Letter to Curtis Bradford*, by the doorbell which was rung by a Boy Scout who should have been at home in bed. However, George said no appreciable harm had been done and soon afterwards we left for a midnight meal.

A year later, Donald inscribed my copy of *A Sequence for Francis Parkman*, the only Listenbook, so far, to be produced: '. . . with pleasant memories of Linton and Cambridge'.

It was shortly after this episode that we were able to buy a Tandberg tape recorder of our own.

When Alison was eleven and Laurien thirteen, George took them on a recording jaunt. I was unable to take the time off work to accompany them. It was the girls' first trip to London and they stayed at our friend Marcus Goodall's flat in Gray's Inn Road. Marcus was much loved by us all and a particular favourite with my daughters. Whenever he visited us in Hessle he invariably brought treats, and always spoke to them as if they were adults.

It was the summer of 1965, George was in holiday mood and on their first day they visited the Tower of London, the Zoo and took a boat trip to Kew Gardens. At night George drove across the different bridges over the Thames, back and forward just for the hell of it, and the lights seemed magical to them.

The next day they drove to Palmers Green to meet Stevie Smith. The girls thought this was great fun since Stevie did not seem to realize how young they were and she too treated them as adults. Accustomed only to lemonade, they were enchanted by the striking woman who poured them large whiskies, offered them cigarettes and cackled merrily. At some point they all tottered off to see her friend, Doreen Diamant, whose name Alison remembered more euphoniously and excitingly as Dorothy Diamond. There was a goat in the back garden and Alison was fascinated by it since she had only ever seen goats in books. This one was eating everything in sight, including tree branches, and she was worried that it would make itself sick.

During the afternoon George made the recording of Stevie reading a selection of her poems and he took some

123

photographs of her for the sleeve. She was very pleased with the record but did not like the cover, and complained bitterly to George for choosing a photograph without first consulting her.

The Whitsun Weddings recording was made in 1964 at Hull University. It took two sessions since there were technical faults on the first tape. I was present at the first session. It was a new departure for us in that Philip introduced his readings with a brief comment on each poem. He decided that a Sunday during the vacation would be the quietest time for our work and we duly met outside the Brynmor Jones Library in the early evening. The empty library was quite eerie as Philip, carrying a big bunch of keys, unlocked a series of doors. He led us up to the top of the building and into an archive room, beautifully sound-proofed by shelves full of ancient parchments and leather-bound tomes. Philip was very well rehearsed. In a business-like manner and with very few hitches he read through *The Whitsun Weddings.* George made the recording. Since I was never allowed to touch the Tandberg, I sat and listened, reflecting on the way Philip's confidence had grown over the last nine years and admiring the great victory he had won over his debilitating stammer. He had also just won the Queen's Gold Medal for Poetry which had sent his popularity soaring and, though he would not admit it, he was clearly very excited by the honour. Twice he stumbled over a line in 'Here': 'And past the poppies bluish neutral distance – Oh ballocks! Do that one again.' (I have noticed that even professional readers seem to have difficulty with this particular cluster of consonants and diphthongs.) He managed to get through it on a third reading and from then on his performance was flawless.

Producing the sleeve was sheer pleasure. As with most of our other records, it illustrated a poem, in this case the title poem which describes a train journey to London at Whitsun with all the newly-married couples climbing aboard to go on honeymoon. Our photograph showed

Philip sitting in a railway carriage looking out of the window with the sun streaming in, making his bald head look less bald. At Paragon Station we had explained our mission and were gratified to have inspectors bowing and scraping and magically clearing the platforms of people. It did occur to us, though, that if they had realized Philip was a poet and not a football star they might not have been so keen to accommodate us.

All the groundwork had been done and we were ready to go ahead when we heard from the record pressers that the stamper of the second side had failed to process so a new master had to be cut. By the time the records were to hand there was still no sign of the sleeves or the wrapping materials. So, as usual, by the time all operations were co-ordinated, we were well over our advertised publication date.

Although Philip was scornful of the navel-gazing school of poetry, he was quite happy to answer our questions about a particular line or an expression that he had used. I remember asking him about the simile of the arrow shower at the end of 'The Whitsun Weddings':

. . . there swelled
A sense of falling, like an arrow shower
Sent out of sight, somewhere becoming rain.

The newly-married couples (and himself, because he is with them) have become partakers in a ritual of regeneration. I wondered how such a strange and powerful image had come to him. Philip said that he had in his mind the scene from Olivier's film *Henry V*, in which the English bowmen shoot at the French and the screen is filled with arrows. That he had taken a visual image concerned with the dealing out of death, and wrested from it such a vivid image of fertility, gave me an interesting insight into the eclectic nature of the poetic imagination.

Fourteen

Pearson Park was built in 1860 by Zachariah Pearson, a rich ship–owner and, at that time, the Mayor of Hull. Although Pearson gave the park to the people of Hull, he reserved the land around it for houses to be built on. It was to one of these three-storeyed houses – number 32 – that Philip had moved in 1958, and he lived there for the next eighteen years. Owned by the University, his red-brick house was one of the more modest buildings that skirted the park. On the opposite curve, across the lawns and beyond the tree-lined pond, the children's play area and the Victorian Conservatory, stood detached mansions built in a variety of architectural styles. Some of them flaunted pillared porches and stone balustrades; too large now to be used as family houses, many of them have been resurrected as private hotels or homes for the aged and one noble edifice called 'Incline', for obvious reasons, has since been demolished and replaced by smart modern flats.

Philip was a good home-maker, as you would expect of a man who was seldom away from home. His attic flat was pretty, the predominant effect being pale pink, the furniture comfortable and chintzy. With his binoculars he had a wonderful view of the park, its trees, birds, children and lovers. His green-fringed eyrie provided the perfect ambience for writing and was obviously the starting point for poems such as 'Toads Revisited', 'The Trees', 'High Windows' and 'Sad Steps'. This last poem is interestingly similar in theme to 'Shut out that Moon' by his beloved Hardy.

During a trip to London in 1964, Philip bought, for several hundred pounds, an oil painting by the Victorian artist, T. F. Marshall (1818-1878). This pastoral scene, in its heavy gilded frame, always had pride of place in his sitting room both at Pearson Park and later at Newland Park. In January 1988 intruders broke into Philip's house and stole the painting along with other valuable property. At first the police were unable to obtain an accurate description of the picture but, fortunately, Ted Tarling had taken a snapshot of it. Prints were distributed among other constabularies; however at the time of writing, the picture has not been recovered.

Philip was anxious about the lack of a fire escape and brooded over the possibility of being roasted alive. The Fire Authority eventually fixed him up with a stout rope which hung on the outside wall near the back window. I am glad he never needed to use it for I could not imagine the unathletic Philip abseiling to the ground from tree top level. Nor could he: 'I'll probably concuss myself on the wall on the way down.'

The thing that most amazed me was the sight, in his bedroom, of three pairs of neatly placed size twelve shoes. Coming from a family of sawn-off, industrial-revolution-type people – my mother wore size three, and those only to accommodate a large bunion – I had thought that shoe sizes stopped at eight.

Contrary to metropolitan opinion, Hull is not a cultural desert. In October 1965 Philip gave a soirée for John Wain who had come to Hull to give a poetry lecture at the University and to stay with him at his Pearson Park flat. Maeve and I attended the reading, expecting John to take up the usual dignified stance at the lectern; instead, he made his eye-boggling entrance with a chair which he fell into with great sighs of exhaustion and brow-moppings. Flicking his long dark hair out of his eyes and complaining about the hazardous nature of train journeys to Hull, substantiated by details which he read out of a British Rail timetable, he proceeded to unload the contents of his bag: two bottles of milk, some oranges and other assorted groceries. I thought they must bear some metaphysical relation to the lecture he was about to give but they remained there unexplained. Perhaps he had been told that Hull was as unprovided for as the Himalayas were.

Afterwards there was an all-male dinner given in his honour (English Society?) so Maeve and I were left behind, in Philip's flat, to prepare party canapès and drinks. Philip had gone to a good deal of unaccustomed expense to equip the sitting-room with extra bookcases and additional articles of furniture in order to impress John. Maeve and I were rather nervous about the expected company which included George, Philip, Wain, Brian Cox of the *Critical Quarterly*, and Geoffrey Moore of the American Studies Department, accompanied by an American professor called Waldhorn. We feared the conversation would be high-powered and excruciatingly intellectual so we put on some of Philip's records and helped ourselves liberally to his bourbon-on-the-rocks. It was just as well we were fortified though it rather blurred the edges of the subsequent happenings.

Very much later than expected, the company arrived clearly in high spirits and minus John whom they had lost somewhere on the way. Philip, the good host as usual, turned on the music and chatted urbanely but was clearly worried about his guest's whereabouts. Maeve and I did the handmaidens of literature bit with the food which they all eyed queasily and refused, having gorged themselves in higher places. Conversation flowed fairly sedately until the door suddenly burst open and John came in wild-eyed and haggard and leaving a trail of dead leaves and twigs. 'I was sick in the park', he said and subsided into a chair. Philip sagged a little and poured more drinks.

Through the mosaic of 'Thanks baby. More ice', and words of wisdom about Saul Bellow, Philip Roth and masturbation, from the American end of the room, I was

128

Me and dad, Withernsea, 1937

Mum and me, Withernsea, 1939

The Wedding Photo, August 1953

Covers of our first and second issues of *Listen*.

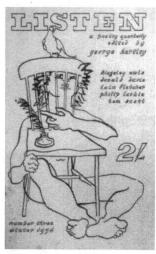

Cover of the third issue of *Listen*.

Cover of *Listen*, Vol.3 No.2, Spring 1959.

Hull Corporation Pier, mid-1950s.

Alison, Jean and Laurien Hartley, 1955

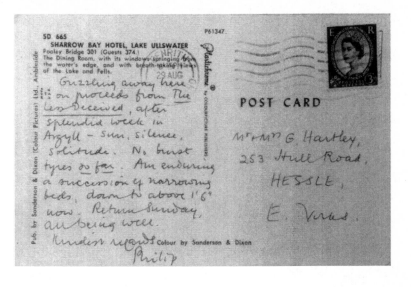

SD 665
SHARROW BAY HOTEL, LAKE ULLSWATER
Pooley Bridge 301 (Guests 374.)
The Dining Room, with its windows springing from
the water's edge, and with breath-taking views
of the Lake and Fells.

P61347.

Guzzling away here
on proceeds from *The
Less Deceived*, after
splendid week in
Argyll — sun, silence,
solitude. No burst
tyres so far. Am enduring
a succession of narrowing
beds, down to about 1'6"
now. Return Sunday,
all being well.
Kindest regards
Philip

POST CARD

Mr & Mrs G. Hartley,
253 Hull Road,
HESSLE,
E. Yorks.

Pub. by Sonderson & Dixon (Colour Pictures) Ltd., Ambleside

Colour by Sanderson & Dixon

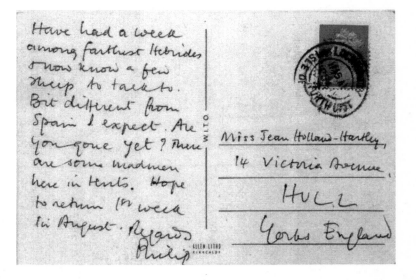

Have had a week
among farthest Hebrides
& now know a few
sheep to talk to.
But different from
Spain I expect. Are
you gone yet? There
are some madmen
here in tents. Hope
to return 1st week
in August. Regards
Philip

Miss Jean Hartley-Hartley,
14 Victoria Avenue,
HULL
Yorks England

Postcards and Christmas card from Philip (and following page)

What a year! Am just about straight, but am about to have arms + legs chopped off (metaphorically) at University.

Hope you are both well!

Merry Christmas and Happy New Year from

Philip

---

32 PPk
10 April 74

I liked the Harvey/Smith card.

Many thanks for invitation for the 27th, which I shall be pleased to accept. Whose birthday is it?

No news. No sign of taking possession of house! Running of family long-distance gardening. Kind regards

Philip

Philip with Ted's painting. Photograph by Ted Tarling

Peter and me on safari

aware that another guest, who had slid to the floor, was propounding some strongly felt truths using Maeve's plates for illustration. Outside, the quiet and moonlit park waited to receive its literary offerings, for John, who was not much of a drinker, had made a number of return journeys and had strewn Philip's carpet with yet more autumn leaves. We watched with fascination as a guest made forcible point after forcible point and one smashed plate after another hit the carpet. Philip winced, wanly placed *Black and Blue* on the turntable and surveyed the ruins, no doubt calculating the 'expense of spirit' and reflecting that John was in no state to appreciate the niceties of the improved household arrangements. This incident did no lasting damage to John and Philip's friendship for about ten years later he was again Philip's guest, for part of the time, when he came to Hull and gave a superb reading at the Spring Street theatre.

In those days there seemed to be a symbiotic relationship between poetry readings and booze which produced tears, fisticuffs or insensibility. William Empson came to the University to give a reading and it was fascinating to hear the familiar lines – bold, lyrical and cryptic as crossword clues – delivered by their begetter. He looked impressively cerebral as he stood at the desk intoning his poems, and his tall, dignified figure had an oddly oriental air. I was intrigued by his white beard which began well under his chin and straggled down his chest like old sheep combings caught on a barbed wire fence. He had clearly been too well fortified for the occasion. As the reading progressed, we watched him slowly sink like the setting sun and finally disappear under the desk.

Philip was happier visiting than entertaining (a trait I have noticed in many bachelors) but the four or five times a year that he did invite us round, we always had a good time. He seldom offered a meal but would lay on savoury snacks such as ham, olives, gherkins and serve lots of drinks. A 1967 entry in my diary outlines one such occasion:

Had marvellous evening playing Armstrong, Fitzgerald, Mr Tambourine Man, etc. Read Rosetti, Conquest, de Vries and talked about Joyce. Reminisced. Philip gave us a poem. Left at 4.0 a.m.

It was during the reminiscing part of the evening, when I had been talking about my schooldays, that Philip said, 'I once wrote a poem about a school,' and produced 'The School in August'. He said that it was written when he was about twenty. I found this surprising since, though the subject and the actual naming of the girl belong to the time when he wrote *Jill*, the cadence and diction seem to belong to his post-Yeatsian style. It lacks the depth he later managed to inject into the least of his poems, however, and it owes much to Betjeman whose work he admired and who was to become his good friend. Before their friendship had ripened, during Philip's illness in 1961, Betjeman asked if he could help him to pay the specialist's fees or meet any other medical expenses. Although Philip demurred, he was deeply touched by this generous gesture.

Philip did occasionally rise to formal entertaining and when C. Day Lewis became Hull University's Poetry Fellow, he gave a dinner in his honour and invited about ten people to The Grange Park Hotel, Willerby. Unused to dining out in restaurants, I felt somewhat overpowered by the occasion especially when one of the guests complained bitterly about the difficulty she had experienced in getting a crate of aubergines flown to her house in time for a special meal she had planned. As I was second senior married woman, Philip sat me on the left of C. Day Lewis whom I found very easy to talk to. He interspersed the literary conversation with helpful hints on etiquette, such as 'Eat the asparagus with your fingers'. Feeling that I would never again have the opportunity, I ordered wild roast boar for my main course. It arrived looking so suspiciously like a Goblin Ready Dinner that I whispered to the waiter, 'Shot it this morning, did you?' 'Tinned', he replied mournfully.

By 1967 it was no longer so necessary for me to work since George, who had obtained a National Diploma in Design and a teaching certificate, was teaching at a local boys' school. Without quite knowing what they were but hearing other people speak highly of them, I decided to pack in my job and take some O and A levels.

I see now how lucky I was to be in my early thirties and free of the burden of looking after tiny children at a time when there was a big expansion in education, and the further education colleges were giving open access to people like me who had missed out on it the first time round. The Hull College of Commerce was thronged with young men who had served in shops or been in dead-end labouring jobs and women, aged from about twenty-five to forty, who were making their bid to escape from domestic servitude. We hoped eventually to obtain interesting and well-paid jobs but that prospect was too misty to speculate about. The important thing was that we were at last getting some directed study rather than keeping lonely vigil at home with Teach Yourself books. When morning lessons were over, we sat in the canteen discussing the works of Chaucer, Shakespeare, Keynes, Adam Smith and Marx over the beans on toast. At the end of term we gathered in the Zoological Arms for hectic farewells. 'What can I drink that's cheap?' I asked a knowledgeable friend. 'Go for an Old Brown' was the reply. Confident, once I had the social formula, I would lean nonchalantly on the bar and ask for an Old Brown until a barman called my bluff by asking, 'an old brown what?'

In sub-standard, and sometimes sub-zero, classrooms in mid-Victorian Board Schools we sat, humble, attentive and full of gratitude for the chance we were being given to learn about demand curves, embourgeoisement or the pathetic fallacy. Unlike some of the younger students, we did not hesitate to answer questions asked by the lecturers;

unfettered at last from stupefying years in factories or kitchens, we jumped in with both feet. We could not have believed then that such expansion would be so shortlived, but these last few years have shown an escalating reduction in the provision of liberal education for adults.

253 was more like Holloway gaol than a home and the girls, aged fourteen and sixteen, bitterly resented the Victorian restrictions placed on them. Occasionally they dared to ask for some of the freedoms their schoolfriends enjoyed. This simply transported them from their pre-vious position as passive onlookers to a place in the firing line. I felt increasingly guilty at keeping them in such an oppressive environment when the marriage was clearly moribund. George spent more and more time out of the house though the same freedoms were not open to me. I struck out by indulging my passion for the cinema, but soon gave this up when I discovered that a woman on her own is a magnet for men in macs. I joined a Scottish country dancing class and found that I had two left legs and no sense of direction. Education was the only answer.

While I was studying I was struck down by a mysterious ailment which caused my joints to swell, particularly my right ankle and shoulder joints. Also a few plaguey black spots appeared on my hand, knee and chin. The illness came on alarmingly quickly for within a few days I could not walk and was admitted to hospital. Philip came at visiting time one Sunday. We talked about the humilia-tions of hospital routine – the endless measuring of what goes into your body and what comes out – and he told me how frightened he had been, six years earlier, when he col-lapsed during a meeting and spent time in hospital being examined by various specialists. He slapped down on my bed an Ed McBain detective novel and a copy of the *News of the World*. 'I thought I'd bring you a *real* newspaper. You probably have plenty of superior crap', he said, looking scathingly at the *New Statesman* and *The Listener*. He was a good sick visitor, relaxed, witty and gentle. Whenever he

132

was ill he described his condition very graphically: 'I feel as though I have a hedgehog in my stomach,' or 'I had that slightly sexy feeling that tells you you're in for a bout of flu.'

I lay there in increasing agony with my joints visibly swelling but was allowed no medication until the disease could be diagnosed. On the tenth day I either heard, or was so delirious that I thought I heard, two doctors talking at the foot of my bed. One of them said to the other, 'We could get a surgeon and saw through the right ankle.' I waited until they had gone then I almost screamed the place down and begged for some treatment. They gave me penicillin and streptomycin injections every few hours. Eventually the swelling diminished and within two or three days I could walk. I thought I had been close to death. Perhaps this made me decide to leave home. It had never been a happy household and for the whole of the next year thoughts of flight were at the back of my mind.

My friends at the College of Commerce, lecturers and students, encouraged me to apply for University. Feeling too embarrassed to ask Philip for a reference, I consulted him over whether I should try Richard Hoggart or Brian Cox. He seemed quite stung at being passed over and said, 'Why not let me do one for you? I've known you long enough. Of course you'll need an UCCA form. UCCA!' he said the word over with relish, 'God's gift to limerick writers: *There was a young lady from UCCA* . . .' I was touched that he came round, after I had taken each of the three A-level English Literature papers, to see how I had done and to talk about the questions.

By the summer of 1968 life had become unendurable, so the girls and I moved out. My association with The Marvell Press ended. I went to see Philip straight away, as I knew he was concerned about the future of his book. Two years earlier, when I had confided to him my troubles and expressed some doubt as to how much longer we would stay with George, his response had been, 'Good God, Jean, what will happen to *The Less Deceived*?' I cannot pretend that martyrdom to the book made me stay but, being a sucker for guilt, it was never far away from my thoughts. I assured him that sales and anthology rights' negotiations were routine and that my book-keeping system could be followed by anyone. He and Monica Jones, his old friend from his Leicester days who was staying with him that weekend, listened to my tale sympathetically and offered advice.

The children and I found an attic flat where we lived for the three years that I was an undergraduate. It had two vast rooms, one of which was L-shaped and doubled as my bedroom and living-room, a kitchen with a dormer window, and (at long last) a bathroom. A fire-escape at the back made a splendid overspill area for parties. My attic was a stone's-throw away from Philip's. As I sat there, writing essays and watching the lime-trees wave through the window I wondered why anyone would want to live in anything other than an attic.

When I began my degree course (the Professor told me during my interview that Philip had given me a glowing reference), Philip said, 'I expect you'll be hard-up living on a grant. I opened a book account for my niece when she went to university. Why don't I do the same for you?' A fortnight later I got a letter from Brown's University bookshop saying that an anonymous donor had opened a £25 account for me. I was very grateful and it helped me enormously in my first year. We needed so much in the way of basic household equipment and I had not even thought about how I might afford to buy the necessary textbooks.

For the first time in our lives there were no restrictions. We could have friends round, go out when we liked, play records, eat what we liked, express our own opinions and renounce subterfuge. We were very hard-up, though our poverty was of a different sort from our previous poverty of the 1950s. And now we had goals. I was determined that

134

the girls should have more choice than I had been given and, in those hopeful days, it seemed education might take a woman a long way towards financial independence. Now, in the grim, post-Thatcherite 90's, it saddens me to look at the bleak faces of young people, qualified or not and from all walks of life, who have no job and not much to look forward to.

It was a great wrench, of course, to leave an enterprise which had filled my life for fifteen years and for which I had worked so hard. It was ironical too that we had reached a modest financial stability: the books and records sold steadily, anthology rights were a lucrative source of income, and we had a substantial archive of letters and manuscripts that could be sold to raise some capital. Even here our views diverged. Being conservative by nature, my plan was to build on the good reputation we had achieved and borrow money to finance some bread-and-butter lines, such as text or reference books, whereas George's plan was to make films. The more excited he became about scripts and hand-held cameras, the more frightened I became and the more determined to leave. The proliferation of little presses proved that shoestring publishing was possible, but I suspected that the streets of London were paved with the bones of back-yard film makers.

Two years after the girls and I left him, George moved to London and communication between us came to an end. He continued to sell the books and records we had produced, but in the next twenty years he published only two new books. While we were married, the profits from the Marvell Press were small. After 1968 and as Philip's reputation grew, the sales of his work increased. Through the courts George fought hard to make sure I would never receive any money from the Marvell Press.

Fifteen

When we had settled in, I invited Philip to my attic flat. Every meal I ever shared with him was prefaced by 'Please may I have my usual glass of water, Jean?' if I happened to forget to provide him with one. He enjoyed the goulash I had made and he told me how simple his own cooking was. Betty, his secretary, had advised him to eat some raw salad every day. This was her prophylactic against catching colds. He had just tried it and promptly caught a cold. One of his most endearing traits was that he would eat anything, or so it seemed. In the old days, at 253, I always tried to provide a choice of cooked meat, pickles and salad in anticipation of his weekend visit. One time I bought a block of marzipan and cut it into chunks, thinking we could eat it for afters. I came out of the kitchen to find him happily eating the marzipan along with his salami and pickled walnuts. He and George were too absorbed in a profound literary conversation for me to interrupt and explain the intended sequence of fare. Was he too polite to comment on the unorthodox mixture and did he complain bitterly to his diary?

'Come to the land of bum' was his appreciative comment on the sight of the three of us in our hippy jeans. Our adoption of miniskirts and 'flares' was symbolic of our liberation from 253 where we wore the nunty tweed suits that George favoured. Philip's own style of dress never changed over the thirty years I knew him. In fact this went further back to judge by photographs of him, at the age of seventeen, wearing a facsimile of the small-check, single-breasted jacket he invariably wore when not at work, the pocket watch on a chain secured to the left lapel.

Philip had reason to feel more than the usual embarrassment a person feels when his or her married friends part company. I was hurt to discover that, as in games of tug-of-war, sides are taken. I collared one erstwhile friend, after he had ignored me numerous times in the street, and asked what I had done to upset him. 'You've stabbed George in the back and bled him dry' was the answer that sent me reeling and wondering what could possibly have given him that idea. All we had done was to leave, quite empty-handed, and move into an unfurnished flat where the three of us were trying to live on one student grant. For months we slept in sleeping-bags on borrowed camp-beds and I cannot remember ever, in the succeeding five years, feeling free of money worries. What I lost in leaving George was considerable. Our household goods may not have been smart but they had taken years to gather and we had an accumulation of books that included many signed first editions. Greater than these, however, was the earning potential of the Marvell Press stock of books and records, and the valuable archive of letters and manuscripts. The friend who was bitter on George's behalf did not understand the difficulty women and children have in laying claim to their dues, for example the £10 a week maintenance for the girls that the court awarded but George never paid. Philip was too fair-minded to be partisan but his Marvell Press contract did put him in an awkward position. Self-interest dictated that he should not, by appearing to be too pally with me, risk antagonizing the person who now dealt with the orders and doled out the royalties. He had once surprised me by saying, 'I *admire* George, but I *like* you.' This was offered as a compliment. I think he meant that he was impressed by George's entrepreneurial skills but that he found me easier to get on with. Towards the end of my marriage Philip began to realize how great was my contribution to the Marvell Press and that I was not just 'the typist'. When, two years after I left him, George moved to London, I sensed that Philip felt easier in his friendship with me.

I chided Philip for not dropping in to see us more often now that we lived so close by. He excused himself by saying, 'You seem to have turned into Beautiful People. I expect you're surrounded by young men playing guitars and smoking pot.' We were, but most of our time was spent swotting – the girls for O and A levels and I for my degree course – and there was constant anxiety about how to make the grant last and where we could find holiday jobs.

Since his illness in 1961 Philip had been rather hard of hearing and over the years this worsened. He was quite open about his disability and he knew that his increasing deafness was a barrier to conversation. He always shuffled round until he got you on his good side – the left – but eventually he had to use two hearing aids. Having lived all my life with a mother who was left with defective hearing after a childhood illness, I knew how isolated he must feel. People are inhibited from saying to the deaf many things that cannot be said at the top of the voice but need a subtle interplay of tones before they can be broached. He said that he had first noticed his deafness when he realized that he could no longer hear the birds sing. Nevertheless, Philip seemed most light-hearted and fulfilled in the 1960s and early 1970s when, despite his habitual irony and self-deprecation, he must have felt potent in two distinct spheres of his public life. As a poet and as a librarian he had done good, solid work for which he was much admired and lauded. The stammer, which had always bedevilled him and which made him shun public speaking, was now under control but he still defended his right to be a private person and refused all requests to lecture, perform at poetry readings, or present the prizes at the local girls' school. Wisely, he viewed such activities as occasions for unnecessary worry and a waste of his precious time. Out-wardly, he must have still seemed to be a publicity-hating recluse (a useful persona for him to adopt) but his friends noticed that, in tune with the times, Philip became more expansive.

Philip sometimes asked me to accompany him to parties, exceedingly dimly-lit affairs where one was ladled a glass of punch and stumbled about a tightly-packed room to the accompaniment of The Stones, Pink Floyd or Stevie Wonder. Through the murk, aspiring young poets would make a bee-line for Philip. His passion for jazz did not exclude an awareness of the current pop scene and he had an affection for the more romantic Beatles numbers. He bought Maeve a copy of 'Yesterday' and played it over and over, the combination of the gin and Paul McCart-ney's voice turning the listeners to sentimental jellies. Gin and the ambience might also account for his claim that Bob Dylan's 'Mr Tambourine Man' was the best song ever written. Perhaps, despite Philip's anti-modernist stance, he was attracted by Dylan's imagist approach to lyric writing and interested to find the influence of Eliot manifest in such an unlikely genre as that of rock music.

Philip kept a paternal eye on my university career and I gave him progress reports when we went out for drinks to village pubs – though pubs were not his favourite places. I imagine that the general hubbub magnified his hearing problem. He said his life changed when he discovered off-licences. He guffawed delightedly when I described the struggle I was having writing my special paper on 'Violent Passion in Early Shakespeare'. The refreshing thing about Philip was that he never thought of trying to impress. By this time his twin careers were gathering for him all man-ner of honours and distinctions but his conversation was free from any kind of boasting. He would much rather give you the latest news about himself via an anecdote in which he ended up with egg on his face. In 1965 he had hoped he would be summoned to the Palace to receive the

Queen's Gold Medal for Poetry and impatiently awaited the call. After a long wait a small packet arrived by registered post and there it was, wrapped in corrugated card. He was similarly disappointed by the Royal Garden Party to which he was invited. He had imagined sitting down to tea with the Royal Family but, instead, he sipped with hundreds, it was hot and sweaty, and Lyons had done the catering. 'Still, it was a good cup of tea.'

In the free air of Victoria Avenue friendships blossomed and the girls and I came to know scores of people. Many of these were brief passengers who left Hull when they had done their stint at the University but some became lifetime friends. Frank Redpath (poet, ex-journalist and, at that time, a third year University student) whom I had known since the old WEA days, and his wife, Mary, came to live in a flat a few doors away from us and lent us lots of essential household equipment including a Baby Belling cooker on which we produced culinary marvels – even Christmas dinners. Rob Watkinson, a young fellow student when I was at the College of Commerce, had done an unspeakably exotic thing and married the French lecturer there; he was now waiting to go to York University. We ate interesting experimental meals at each other's homes on alternate weekends and, after supper, Rob would sing for us in his wonderfully resonant voice, 'Shoals of Herring', 'The Durham Lockout', some Jacques Brel songs or the latest Bob Dylan and Van Morrison numbers. Life was rich.

Life was not without its tensions though. The girls and I had left 253 precipitately and had only the clothes we stood up in. Friends had helped out magnificently but there were things we needed and my solicitor suggested I ask George for our personal effects and a portion of the family goods. I explained to him that such share-outs might work with other families but not with ours. So on a day when I knew George to be at school, I set off for 253, armed with a solicitor's card and with Frank Redpath for support.

The key was useless for the locks had been changed. We sidled round the back to see if any windows were unlatched. Finding the upper bedroom window open, I went down the garden to fetch a ladder which Frank gallantly volunteered to scale. By now our hearts were pounding and Frank missed his footing when spooky Mrs Deasle, from next door, appeared in her backyard looking like an illustration from a Mervyn Peake novel. 'Just collecting a few of our things', I called to her cheerily as we watched Frank's ample behind wrestle its way into the bedroom. Once inside, I was overcome by sadness and apathy. Here were the relics of fifteen years' worth of family life. Apart from love and loyalty, they were the things that had kept me there: the madras bedspread, the sweetcorn design curtains that had been such a bargain and the litter of books. Feeling like an interloper, and guilt-ridden at not having managed to make the marriage work, I gathered together items that were indisputably ours: my face-cream and slippers, Laurien's ballet books, Alison's collection of seedy teddy-bears. I was leafing through old photographs when Frank came through and asked me about the stuff I wanted to take. 'These', I said pointing to the pathetic assortment. 'You'll not get far in life with only your curlers and hot-water bottle. What about this Hoover and some pillows', he said, directing me to more practical objects. In retrospect I see how over-scrupulous and naïve Frank and I were. There were bookcases full of signed first editions; Philip had inscribed to both of us all of his books including the rare and valuable *XX Poems*. There was a suitcase full of signed first editions of Robert Graves publications and other similar collections, not to mention the Henry Moore and Patrick Heron original signed drawings. If I had taken the Marvell Press manuscript collection I would have assured myself of at least a small stake in the joint finances and gained the power to bargain for a share in the ongoing profits.

Opening a drawer I came across the pistol that had

belonged to my brother, Harry, which had doubtless been given to him by one of his ex-service friends and kept as a war memento. I once inadvisedly mentioned the weapon to George and, in 1955, after Harry had left Hull to go to New Zealand, George pestered me to get it for him. I did and it had lain in his drawer ever since. Harry returned to Hull in 1958 but never alluded to his loss. We were not on the sort of terms where he could make such a curious conversational opener as, 'I once had this gun in my sock drawer and it's disappeared. This is just a shot in the dark but I don't suppose you'd know . . . ?' Frank looked at the offensive object, stopped in his tracks, and said 'Christ! Whose is this?' When I told him, he decided it wasn't something you want to leave lying around, and put it in his inside pocket. We carried on sorting through piles of stuff. 'Jean, do you want the typewriter?' 'No I bloody don't,' I said, thinking of my years of bondage to it. That was a foolish decision for six years elapsed before I could afford a cheap portable model.

Suddenly a great cacophony broke out at the front of the house. The door was wrenched open and we were confronted by a plain-clothes detective, two police officers, George's mother and Mrs Deasle. A great deal of fast talking and explanation ensued, counterpointed by George's 'grim head-scarved' mother's vehement language. Her strong Scottish accent added power to her delivery: 'She's got no frigging right to anything in this house . . . This is my son's house and she's no better than a bloody whore . . . She'd had one bairn before he married her.' Ignoring this, the detective interposed himself between the warring parties and addressed me and Frank. 'Now then, madam. What is your name? And who are you, sir?' 'I am an old friend who is helping Mrs Hartley to reclaim some of her property,' said Frank, in his best magisterial manner. 'And can you show me any authority for this intrusion?' countered the policeman. 'Of course,' Frank confidently asserted, fishing in his inside pocket for the solicitor's card but first encountering cold metal.

I had forgotten about the gun and, seeing the sweat instantly break out on his brow, put it down to the stress we were both feeling at the melodramatic turn the event had taken. Mrs Deasle's recitative could be heard in the background: ' . . . ladder . . . smashed their way in . . . thought I'd better telephone . . .' And in the foreground was George's mother who had now turned her histrionics towards my accomplice: 'He's no better than a burglar.' Frank triumphantly produced the solicitor's card and, under police protection, we were allowed to hump the bedding and bits and pieces to the car. This was the ultimate delectation for the neighbours who, having been starved of excitement in the months since I had left, now provided a dramatic chorus to the last act. Mother-in-law was still on top-note so I took a policeman aside and explained to him that she suffered from a heart condition and should be accompanied home. Mind you, for a supposedly sick woman she had done quite well that day and in the past had not been noted for giving the soft answer that turneth away wrath, though she did mellow over the next ten years.

Panting and drained we drove back with our booty, Frank exclaiming, 'Good God, Jean! I had *no* idea your life was like that. You put up such a good front. Why didn't you leave years ago?' Then, 'Bloody hell! What shall I do with that ditch-begotten gun? Oh well, I'll think of something. I can't have watched all those gangster films for nothing.' For the next few weeks we speculated about what to do with it. We could take it to the police but the truthful explanation would be complicated and unbelievable. A trusted friend offered to hide it in a cupboard, and there it stayed until her husband, uncharacteristically, became violent. It then seemed wise to remove it. One night a party of conspirators drove to the pier, made a furtive reconnaissance for hidden policemen, smoked a few cigarettes, then, feeling like fugitives from a B film, dropped it in the Humber.

Now that we had some of our old and treasured possessions about us, we began to feel more at ease in our new situation. The girls did not neglect their school work but they took full advantage of their first chance to have a social life of their own.

Alison had fallen in love with The Incredible String Band – a pop group which produced a fey blend of folk and rock music. They were the epitome of Flower Power in their Indian cottons, headbands, stove-pipe hats and gentle injunctions to their audiences to hold hands or be happy. I felt I knew more about Robin, Mike and Licorice than I did about Beowulf, Sir Gawain and Moll Flanders about whom I was supposed to be writing essays. Whenever Alison had saved or scrounged a bit of money she squandered it on an Incredible String Band record or concert ticket. The only way I could think of being sure she was safe, as she hared around the country paying her devotions to them, was to go with her. The alternative was to sit through long, nail-biting nights waiting for her to get home. I once got a telephone call at 2.30 a.m: 'Hello, Mum. I thought you might be worried so I've just rung to say I'm in Liverpool and I've missed the last train but I've met these nice men in embroidered velvet cloaks who say I can stay at their place.' Click went the phone before I could reply. So I became an unwilling String Band fan. Train fares were usually beyond our resources and it seemed safe to hitch as there were two of us. Alison would wait at the roadside and I would conceal myself behind a bush until a car or lorry slowed down. As she was getting in I would leap after her with caftan flapping and beads clanking painfully against my chest.

The subject of Laurien's passion was nearer home and easier to satisfy. I used to queue up for free tickets to the University Drama department's productions and, after seeing *Little Malcolm and his Struggle against the Eunuchs*, Laurien declared undying love for Gareth, its star. Whenever he was to appear, she would zoom off to the

University on her bike, fair hair flying in the wind, and would come back after the performance sighing contentedly. (Hull is a great place for push bikes because the land is very flat and the roads straight.) There was one memorable evening when Laurien rushed in crying, 'He spoke to me! He actually spoke to me!' 'What did he say?' I asked, thinking he must at least have made a date with her. 'Well, I was late so I pedalled like hell then, as I was going down that slope near the Green Room, I put the brakes on but they wouldn't work and I ran straight into him. I said, *Oh I am sorry*, and he said [here Laurien looked rapturously into the middle distance] *Oh, that's all right . . .* and he *smiled* at me.' He was more likely wincing with pain, but the convergence of the twain buoyed her up for weeks after.

Sixteen

The house which contained our flat had been sold to a rather unsociable neighbourhood couple. We, as sitting tenants, were in their way and they began a relentless campaign of harassment to get us out. They would turn the electricity off, lock us out, fill our dustbins and hiss like geese when they met us in the street. I was swotting for finals, wondering how I could afford to get Laurien kitted out for Newcastle university, and doing battle with the headmaster of the comprehensive school Alison attended – this was about her supposed peccadilloes – so I had not much energy left for fighting the neighbours. In the words of Empson, 'it seemed the best thing to be up and go.'

Further down the avenue there was a two-storey house with lovely, light, semi-circular bay-windows and a front garden full of sunflowers. Once I stopped to tell the owner how much I admired the flowers. He told me that he and his wife were leaving Hull and suggested that I might like to buy the house. George had moved to London and there was now, after years of long and painful litigation, some possibility that I might be awarded a half-share of the money made on the sale of the marital home. In the hope that this would soon come to pass and thus enable me to take out a mortgage, we moved into number 82 Victoria Avenue.

That same autumn of 1972, after having graduated, I was accepted to read for the B.Phil. degree. It comprised a year's taught course in Victorian thought and literature, culminating in a three-paper examination and a 15,000 word dissertation on a subject of one's own choice. I chose to write about the work of John Meade Falkner, a quirky, late-Victorian writer who most people know of through reading his novel, *Moonfleet*. I had hoped this would be a satisfying year and that I could study selected writers in greater depth than had been possible in the tightly-packed B.A. course. In fact, it took us on an even madder gallop through the annals of Eng. Lit. and Phil. than I could ever have imagined. In an average week we were required to read, and prepare a seminar paper on, two fat novels – say, a Trollope and a Thackeray. Granted, I am a slow reader, but even allowing myself a bare six hours sleep a night and minimal sandwich breaks, I usually finished the second novel with five minutes to spare before the seminar and, by then, the characters and action of both novels had become inextricably intermingled in my addled brain.

Given a modicum of help from my supervisor and a few more weeks in which to write it, I think I could have made a decent job of the dissertation; as it was, I felt deeply dissatisfied with it. A few weeks after I had submitted it, I saw Philip driving in stately fashion down the Avenues. He wound down his car window and congratulated me, saying how much he had enjoyed reading the piece. I knew the subject would have been congenial to him for he included three poems by Falkner in his *Oxford Book of Twentieth-Century English Verse*, but I could not help feeling that he was being kind in praising what I knew to be thin work and ill-considered scholarship. Time was short because I had misunderstood the terms on which the £600 B.Phil. grant was offered. I imagined I would be able to research and write it during the summer while drawing social security. By the end of the third term, after I had spent the whole inadequate sum and more, I discovered that it had been given for a calender and not an academic year. A single student could have got by on it but with two adolescent girls and a house to keep, it went nowhere. In emergencies I borrowed from my mother and brother but they were not well off so I needed to find other ways of eking out the grant. Since I had a three and a half bed-roomed house, taking in lodgers seemed to be the answer.

From the day we moved in we had established bed-sitters for ourselves so sharing the house would be no hardship. My domain was the front downstairs room with my bed rather unsafely placed against a wall that bore three long, sagging bookshelves; the three other white walls were broken up by cheese plants, scented geraniums and posters. John, who worked at the University, rented the front bedroom and used the adjacent boxroom as his kitchen. He was clean, tidy, paid on the dot and offered me the use of his television set. Alison had the middle bed-room, a joss-stick-smelling cave full of Man, Myth and Magic magazines, the walls festooned with String Band, Bob Dylan and Richard Dadd posters. Conversation with her was not easy since whenever I ventured in she was either transcendentally meditating or standing on her head practising yoga. Laurien's room at the back of the house was empty during term time when she was at Newcastle studying French.

One day John asked me if I would take in a young Middle Eastern student who was homeless and needed a quiet room to work in. At first I refused but the circum-stances sounded so pitiful that I relented and said I would see him. All charm and white teeth, Halid bulldozed me into accepting him, squeaked with delight at the back bed-room and moved in the next day. I had no spare key so I lent him mine and asked him to get one cut since I was busy revising. Next day I was halfway through Trollope's *The Way We Live Now* when I became aware of unmis-takable humping noises emanating from the back bedroom. Didn't know you could do it on your own, I thought, and then, perhaps he's weight lifting, and went back to my book. An hour later I was on my way to the bathroom when a sleek imperious blonde girl pushed past me and slammed the door in my face.

Later that evening, I was in the family sitting-room when Halid barged in and said that the back bedroom was unbearably poky for two people and he would like to add the room we were in at present to his suite. I nodded sympathetically and was half inclined to agree until I remembered that I had rented the room to one, not two. 'Sorry. Can't do', I insisted during the half hour of his alternate wheedling and bullying and 'Where's my key?' I yelled after him as he flounced out. 'I've been too busy. I'll do it tomorrow', he answered. I can scarcely believe that for the next week I sat on the front doorstep reading for hours, on and off, waiting for someone to come home and let me in. Only an overriding preoccupation with Victorian poets and thinkers can account for it.

The last straw came when John tapped on my door and very hesitantly asked if I had borrowed a chicken and various other comestibles from his fridge. 'I don't mind if you have,' he said, 'but I'd just like to know.' We put two and two together and came up with Halid. I placed a note under his door asking him to leave at the end of the week. He put one under mine saying no he would not and that it would be the worse for me if I tried to make him go. A bit of detective work put us on to his tutor who said that Halid had lots of problems and was undergoing an identity crisis. 'Who does he think he is – Genghis Khan?' I shrieked. The tutor earnestly explained that Halid was under a great deal of pressure from his father, a high-ranking official but he would try to reason with him and would get in touch with him at his student house. This was the first I had heard of any alternative accommodation (he had obviously chosen my house as his love-nest), so I asked for the address. Between then and the weekend I did not see or hear him in the house but I received a number of abusive telephone calls so I assumed that he had decamped to the student house with my key.

Unnerved by this time, and wondering if it had all been worth the four quid I had so far received, I asked Frank if

149

he would help me to move Halid's gear and, on Saturday morning, my friend Helen and I nervously broke into the back bedroom. What a mess! Curtains drawn, electric fire left on! We found his suitcases and packed his belongings. Helen's nose wrinkled with disgust as she shifted half empty food cartons off the bed and gathered up sheets stuck together with bread and jam. Downstairs, Ali's large friend, Keith, and my brother Harry, had dropped in and were being pressed to swell the loading party. Mafia-like, the five of us piled into the Rover with the cases and swept off to Cranbrook Avenue. Frank had psyched himself up to do the tough bit and he and I went to the door. After knocking on it he said to me, 'What's Halid's surname?' I searched my memory and finally came up with 'Dargoosh'. With that the door opened and a defensive-looking Halid appeared. 'Are you Halid Dargoosh?' Frank asked in his most authoritative voice. At that moment I remembered that I had not been able to decipher Halid's surname on the cheque he had given me, and that Dargoosh was the name of the curry I had eaten in Bradford three weeks earlier. My hand went forward to tap Frank on the shoulder and recant but it was too late. 'Yes', said Halid, too terrified, I suspect, to deny it. 'I understand you have been harassing Mrs Hartley and have refused to leave her premises.' The back-up mob sat in the Rover looking aggressive as Frank gave Halid his suitcases, extracted my key and warned him not to pester me again.

But he did. All that night, every couple of hours the telephone rang and (too canny to let me hear his voice) the heavy breathing began. I finally dropped off to sleep but at 3 a.m. it rang again. I picked up the receiver, swore some unrepeatable oaths into the mouthpiece, put it down, slammed the door of my room and found that I had left my thumb in it. Pulling the covers over my head to muffle the howls of pain, I decided that landladying was not my forte. Word got round some weeks later that it would be wise for us not to try to cross certain national borders.

Chance would have been a damned fine thing. Somehow we got through that year. During the summer, when I had hoped to be free to write the dissertation, I did a succession of temporary jobs by day and my writing at night until, in September, I found permanent work.

A week after the beginning of the autumn school term, and by the skin of my teeth, I got a job at Amy Johnson High School. Oddly enough, this was my old school, Thoresby, rebuilt, renamed and changed into a smart, purpose-built, girls comprehensive. The vacant post was occasioned by the retirement of Miss Senior, my erstwhile English teacher. A well-qualified man from out of town had been appointed to the job at the end of the previous term. He had inspected the school, declared himself satisfied but failed to appear when term started. On the third day he telephoned to say his wife did not want him to make the move. By that late date I must have been the only English graduate on the Education Committee's books, so they snapped me up. Everything I have ever done in life I have felt scared of and unprepared for but never more so than then. I had three days in which to achieve the metamorphosis from student to teacher.

I doubt if I would have survived without Molly Rotheray, a beautiful, ever-young woman in her early fifties who was loved and revered by the girls and the staff. Molly was a 'Girton girl' with high intellectual standards and a sense of humour that carried me through horrendous afternoons with 3TN and chaotic improvised drama sessions that I had no idea how to control. Lunch time with Molly in the cosy 6th form staffroom where we munched our peanuts, cheese and apples, ameliorated the defeat of the morning and fortified me for the battle in the afternoon. Wreathed in smoke, we talked about T. S. Eliot, T strap shoes, my abortive love life, her East End childhood and what strategy could be used to hold down 5TN for long enough to get them to put pen to paper. She told me about her first teaching experience when she arrived in

151

Hull as a novice. The teacher in the staffroom had pointed to the simmering kettle, said 'Mash the tea when it boils' and whizzed out, leaving Molly to wonder exactly what it was these barbaric northerners did to their tea. Finding no mashing implement she sat there panic-stricken and impotent until the teacher returned, tutted at her ignorance and *brewed* up.

My first year was also the first year of the Raising of School Leaving Age to sixteen. The ROSLA girls; the euphonious sound bears no relation to the noise which quite understandably emanated from girls who, mature in body and infinitely more streetwise than their GCE stream contemporaries, were impatient at being clawed back into school when they could have been out earning their own money in the shops and factories of Hessle Road. Resentful at having to wear uniforms and keep rules, they sabotaged our thoughtfully constructed lessons by imposing their own culture: Gary Glitter posters, Bay City Rollers magazines, scarves, badges, and double page spreads on the Osmonds filled their heads and littered the classrooms, making it difficult for us to keep to the narrow brief imposed on us by the headmistress.

Molly made sure that the ROSLA burden was shared fairly and that each member of the English department received a leavening of GCE class work (little islands of academic enterprise, with groups of bright-eyed, motivated daughters of parents who were keen that their girls should 'get on'). Molly also rigorously but gently tried to keep the less self-disciplined of her department from sinking into a mire of disorder. At one of her weekly departmental lunchtime meetings she addressed us, her usual sweet smile tempered by an uncompromising eye: 'I know you're all pushed for time, but I would be grateful if you could bring your forecast books in so that I can have a look at them over the weekend.' Six blank, uncomprehending gazes met hers. 'What's a forecast book, Molly?' I ventured, thinking my greenness would excuse my ignorance. 'The book in which you write down your lesson plans for the coming week, then give an account of how each one actually went, followed up by an analysis of how the lesson could have been improved' she answered matter-of-factly. We had all turned a whiter shade of pale and, saved by the bell, slunk out into the heaving corridor, wondering how we could ever live up to our paragon or manage quickly to fake up a plausible set of forecasts from scruffy notes made hastily on the backs of envelopes.

I made good friends there – Romie, Deirdre and, not least, Angela, whose name and title the headmistress rolled appreciatively round her tongue on every possible occasion – Dr Platt this, Dr Platt that – for she was her prized and only Ph.D. (I expect the school is wick with them now that job opportunities for higher graduates have so sadly diminished.) But I really wanted to move. Going back to teach at your old school is too much like stepping back in time; also, memories of the happy two years I had spent at the College of Commerce made me hanker after doing that sort of work. I wanted to teach adult students.

Angela had become my lodger for a term. Her character was a combination of the visionary and the practical and she put her scientific mind to the reorganization of the Hartley household for the greater good of the inhabitants – at that time just me and her. On Fridays Deirdre would drive us home from school and by 4.30 Ange and I had gathered up the dirty washing and were on Newland Avenue. There we dumped the washing in the laundrette, then bought something like: two pieces of fish, a pound of mince, two kippers, two pork chops, eight sausages, a pound of squid and an assortment of fruit, veg. and groceries (a protein item was taken out of the freezer compartment of the fridge each morning to defrost for the evening meal). After we had stowed away this haul, we thoroughly cleaned the house, mucked out and fed the cats, picked up the clean washing, ate a meal, washed our hair, had baths and were lounging in the Queen's drinking halves of lager by 8.30. What order! Life has never been the same since that Christmas when Angela went to Gloucester to marry Pete.

I celebrated my fortieth birthday while I was at Amy Johnson High School. It was a landmark which, for some reason, I had not expected to reach. I had a meeting with myself, to use a phrase my brother is fond of, and decided that there should be a man in my life but I found there were very few suitable customers on the market. Most of the really nice men I knew were, understandably, deeply married. The ones who were single seemed to be chancers, emotional leeches or barflies. Where do you meet acceptable single men when you are forty? I did not fancy bopping off to Romeo and Juliet's disco or going to a singles club and the one or two good men I had met over the years had expectations of me that were quite unrealistic. There was my cycling friend for example. He worked at a killing job in a caravan factory for three months of each year in order to finance himself on tours of different continents for the other nine months. He had already done Europe, North America and the Middle East. His next project was South America and he proposed buying a tandem so that I could accompany him. I could not see myself pedalling behind him over the Andes in shorts, and what would happen to my cats?

After much pragmatic discussion of the man problem in the staffroom, I decided to join a dating agency, paid my twenty quid and apprehensively awaited the result. Would it be like the postal trousers that were too big in the seat or like the socks I ordered from the catalogue firm that sent me babies mittens instead? Yes, it was rather.

There was clearly not much in stock to suit a forty year old for I only received two names and addresses. The first turned out to be a pleasant woodwork teacher from Sheffield. He drove over to Hull a couple of times a week and we visited stately homes, exclaiming together over the Chippendale chairs and the Grinling Gibbons grapes. We would round off the day with steak meals at inns on the outskirts of the town. All was going smoothly until the evening when I asked him what he wanted from life. 'Six children' he replied. After I had finished choking over my Black Forest gateau I told him, as gently as possible, that it was a little late for me to embark on that kind of empire building. The next candidate was a big game hunting accountant from Leeds. He talked all night about the thrill of the chase and the kill, apparently quite deaf to my repeated wails of, 'But I stated quite clearly on the form that I didn't approve of bloodsports.'

I felt nothing but relief when two months had elapsed and no further suitors were forthcoming. Then one day a computer slip arrived with a local man's name and address on it. I duly wrote and suggested that he call for me at 7 p.m. and that we go for a drink.

The door bell rang at ten to seven. Ardent or just a good time-keeper, I wondered. My first thought when I saw the man who stood on the doorstep was that he looked just like my brother. My second thought was, it *is* my brother. It flashed briefly through my mind that Harry was a pseudonymous customer of the dating agency but I was quickly reassured when he said, 'I wasn't sure if I'd find you in.' 'Well', I replied, 'I'm almost on my way out. You see, I thought you were the man I'm expecting. The fact is, I've sent away for a bloke.' I was really embarrassed by this time for, when put on the spot, I am never quick-witted enough to think of a face-saving lie. So I burbled on: 'After all, if you wanted a pound of carrots, you'd go to a greengrocer, wouldn't you? So I joined this dating agency. The selection's not been much cop up to now but the latest one's due to turn up in ten minutes.' I could not but admire the aplomb with which Harry digested and accepted this rigmarole. He carefully fastened his bike lock and said: 'Righto then, dear. I won't hold you up. I'll just leave you this haddock. I've had two pounds of it given and there's too much for us to eat so I've brought you half of it. It's nice and fresh. Put it in the fridge while I go and dig up a tinful of worms out of your compost heap. Fishing season starts this week. Then I'll get off out of your way.'

Ten minutes later the date arrived and we appraised each other through narrowed eyes. I had grown accustomed to these Mexican stand-offs. He was bowler-hatted, business suited, carrying a brolly and a rolled copy of *The Times*. Another accountant? I was wearing my ruched, three-tiered, patchwork, ankle-length skirt, a second-hand fur coat and about ten strings of beads. It boded ill from the start. During the evening it became apparent that he required a replacement for his recently deceased mother. Later that night I decided that the celibate life was preferable to the rigours of the dating agency.

After two years of working at Amy Johnson, I had paid off all my debts and was able to take my first real holiday since 1967. Laurien was in the second term of her assistant-ship at Château-du-Loire, a small market town between Tours and Le Mans. She invited Alison, my friend Margaret and me to spend Easter there. Pascal, the local vet's son, a mature lad for his fifteen years and a pupil of the school where Laurien taught, had fallen deeply in love with her and offered to take us out while Laurien was teaching. He would appear at the Hotel de la Gare in the mornings, just as we had haltingly ordered breakfast from the black clad and dignified madame. There was a frightening incongruity between her poker-backed rectitude and the postcard stand which flanked her and which contained the dirtiest examples of the art I had ever seen: graphic line drawings displayed cavorting naked couples with their pox-ridden bums well to the foreground – quite different from the cheerful chamber-pot vulgarity of their English counterparts.

I think Pascal was quite proud to tote the three Anglaises – four when Laurien could join us – round the cafés, the shops and the benign spring countryside. On one memorable day, we had a picnic at his father's *cave* – these natural formations in the rocky outcrops were converted to giant cellars by the locals and cool, dark and dry, the bottles rested on ledges cut into the rock. In front of the *cave*, Pascal set up a brazier, cooked steaks for us and produced some of his father's choice vintages. After the bleak Hull spring weather and the rigours of the Amy Johnson school, it was blissful to be able to eat outside in a landscape full of apple blossom and flowering vineyards. A small boy came out of the fields and wandered up to us holding a string of brightly coloured adders on a stick. Pascal explained that he had caught them and was taking them to the hospital where he could sell the venom which would be made into serum. The whole fortnight was crowded with such languorous, golden days, each one like a plate from the Duc de Berry's *Très Riches Heures*.

That Christmas, the next and the next, Pascal came to Hull, bearing wine, champagne and flagons of scent specially chosen by his handsome father to match our individual auras. M. Jeanjot had also urged his son to make sure we were regularly supplied with flowers and chocolates during the fortnight's holiday. When the lad arrived I was nervous and I rather thoughtlessly greeted him with, 'Do come in, Pascal, and divest yourself of your baggages.' He looked dumbstruck and Laurien said, 'For God's sake, mum! He didn't learn his English from Dickens.' I was careful after that, shouting every word distinctly in the way that non-French-speaking English people invariably do.

Pascal was at home in the kitchen and we all mucked in to cook the Christmas dinner. We even took photographs of it. I was especially proud because I had, for the first time, with the well-named Angela, made the cake and the pudding. My mother had always done this for me in the past but now her health was failing and it was my turn to do this service for her as well as for myself. Pascal loved the whole meal but he moaned with particular pleasure over the Christmas pudding, rich, brandy haloed and so very English. 'What is in it?' he asked between mouthfuls and we gave him the litany of 'brazil nuts, glace cherries, demerara sugar, muscatel raisins,' etc. 'And what is this?' he asked more doubtfully, displaying the contents of his spoon for identification. I blushed deeply and answered, 'That is a fag-end, Pascal, Players No. 6 tipped. I can't think how it got there but please don't tell your mother.' I could imagine the kindly but bourgeois Jeanjots sitting erect in their high-backed chairs and feeling that they had cast their gifts as pearls before a swine.

In April 1974 I invited Philip to my birthday party. He came bearing a present of Creme de Menthe. 'Put it away quickly before some bugger swigs it,' he advised. It was his first visit to my new house and his greater-than-usual interest in the decor betrayed his preoccupation with the Newland Park house that he was in the process of purchasing. He had not yet taken possession of it but said that he had done 'plenty of long-distance gardening.' It seemed to me perverse that he chose an ugly little house that he didn't much like when he could have bought an upper storey flat or a beautiful house with an attic to disappear up to. After all, money was no object. Philip expressed great surprise that my house was fully furnished. 'How on earth do you manage it?' he asked. 'I'm having endless trouble and, oh, the expense!' He did not know about friends' throw-outs and Victoria's Emporium, a wonderful second-hand shop where you could get four chairs, a table and a fur coat for five pounds. Everything Philip bought was at full price, of good quality and carefully considered. Years earlier there had been endless deliberation before he purchased his Pye Black Box and his Rollieflex Camera. I watched him chatting amiably to my friends and he seemed to be getting on well with them but afterwards he confided to Ted Tarling that he was worried about me: 'Did you know that Jean is mixing with Revolutionaries?' He must have been referring to one or two Labour Party members to whom I had introduced him.

His political naïvety always astounded me but I suppose he was simply not interested in politics and so it was easy to adopt the bluff conservatism that must have been handed down to him by his parents and shared by his friends at school and at Oxford. I say this because I always found him fair-minded, scrupulous and warm-hearted in his personal dealings. To me, the general blimpishness and insensitivity to the plight of others less fortunate than himself was a mask he wore to ward off issues that he did not want to have to think about. When I asked him round for a meal he would sometimes say: 'You won't invite any left-wingers who'll bully me, will you?'

In the early days of our friendship the subject had never arisen until Philip arrived one day, after a general election, rejoicing over a Conservative victory. I told him we always voted Labour and that I could not imagine how any person who had to work for a living could vote otherwise. An emotional scene ensued during which we each voiced our gut reaction to the other's views. 'I have to be a socialist out of sheer self-preservation. A hundred years ago my counterpart would have been sent up chimneys or had to scrub someone else's floors from dawn to dusk as my mother did.' He shrugged disbelievingly and eased his jacket out of the iron-pronged chair which always managed to trap him. Socialism, for Philip, was on a par with modern jazz – a descent into chaos. Eventually we had a tacit agreement not to discuss politics.

I think, though, that we both really belonged to that insular group of English people who cling to a class-inherited political stance and are too preoccupied with their own narrow interests to take an active part in the outside world: the Jane Austen syndrome. People like us work in offices during the day, do the shopping at lunchtime and maybe get to the library. During the tea-break we might glance at a newspaper but, more likely, we will chat to a colleague about office politics. In the evening, for Philip, there would be the stanza to complete or the *Daily Telegraph* jazz review to map out. For me there would be the meal to prepare and clear, then the essay to write. Presidents are assassinated, men walk on the moon and there is horror in Vietnam. It all registers, but three hundred years separate us from our many-faceted Renaissance ancestors and many more years have passed since England was last invaded by an enemy. Our literature – Dickens and Orwell are two of the few exceptions – reflects the lack of commitment to wider concerns and an acceptance of the restricted view.

Philip always spoke very fondly of his mother whom I met only once. She looked, of course, very different from the early photograph of her, which he carried in his wallet, that showed her wearing a large Edwardian toque. The glimpses of her he gives us in 'Love Songs in Age' and 'Reference Back' reveal his understanding of her and his affection for her. It was sad and worrying for him when, in 1972, she was taken, after having had a fall, to a nursing home to be looked after. Philip's belief in the value of love, in its widest sense, was not only implicit in all he wrote but also in his way of life. In her last years he wrote to his mother every day and he regularly travelled to Loughborough to see her. His reverence for the bonds that tie us to one another is shown with great clarity in his seaside idyll 'To the Sea'. Here in a skilful blend of the personal and the universal, he affirms the need for reciprocal caring: 'teaching their children by a sort/ Of clowning; helping the old, too, as they ought.' His mother died in 1977 at the age of 91.

My own mother died in the same year, a few months before her eightieth birthday. Her life had not been an easy one, yet I never once heard her complain. In 1919 at the age of twenty-one, she left domestic service in order to nurse her mother, a widow, who had become bedridden with rheumatism. While in service, my mother had joined the Suffragette Movement but there was not much chance of her being active in it once she had her invalid mother and a family of six to look after. Three of the ten children were grown up, married and out of the nest but the rest were still at home and my Aunt Madge – the last of the litter, born when her mother was menopausal – was only eight. Mum told me that as a youngster she had been a real tomboy; I suspect that the six years she spent caring for her mother, brothers and sisters, before she married my dad, must have knocked the bounce out of her.

My mother's going was a protracted one: it lasted two years. Having ruled by routines, she gradually mixed up the routines, withdrew from the outside world and embarked on a huge forgetfulness. On Thursday at 12.30 p.m. she and Harry had sausages for lunch but now the sausages might be burnt black, or sitting raw in the pan with no light under them, or she might still be wandering up the road looking for the shop from which she had bought sausages for the last sixty years. In her lifetime she had scrubbed clean a succession of dirty faces, bandaged innumerable cut knees and fed so many open mouths. Harry and I found it hard to accept that the little boss was no longer capable of taking charge even of herself, never mind of anyone else.

There were some few months agonizing overlap between the onset of mother's senility and C. D. Holmes making Harry redundant. The redundancy came as a mixed blessing. Although the loss of his job, and the income that went with it, was distressing, he was relieved to be at home to look after Mum and make sure that she did not harm herself. The firm did not run a pension scheme for its tradesmen and all Harry received for his thirty five years of service was £1,500 severance pay. During the next six months he spent £800 of it, plus my mother's old age pension, on living expenses since the state refused to pay him either unemployment or social security benefit.

161

There were medical problems too. The fact that Mum no longer enjoyed reading, we found, was because she had cataracts in her eyes and could not see. When she suddenly became incontinent, a new bed had to be bought and the old one thrown away. At the height of all this trouble, a nurse called and told Harry that mother was diabetic and would need a special diet. She was reeling off a list of requirements when Harry, at the end of his tether, interrupted her to say, 'Look dear, I'll deal with all this tomorrow but just now I think you'd better go.' His endless rounds of the Government agencies in pursuit of weekly benefits, had finally met with, 'I'm afraid, Mr Holland, there is no legislation that covers your case.' 'Does that mean, then, that I'm in the gutter?' Harry asked. 'It looks that way' was the smug reply.

One day, when Harry's frustration and despair had mutated to fury, he marched off to the Social Security office, demanded to see the manager, and said to him, 'If you don't come up with some funds, pronto, I shall bring this old lady, with her clothes, and leave her in your office for you to look after. I shall then shut up the house, take my cat and book myself into a boarding house.' This produced instant action. Harry received a cheque for £50 back-pay by the next post and was from then on besieged by an army of do-gooders bearing, somewhat belatedly, rubber sheets, commodes and the like. Some of them, though, just came to do their book-keeping exercises. One man sat for an hour asking personal questions and filling in complicated graphs. At the end of his labours he announced triumphantly, 'Your mother has just qualified for twenty four more points.' 'What does that mean – Bingo?' Harry asked. 'No, it means she's due for an extra 12½ pence a week.' 'That's about a bar of soap to us,' Harry replied, 'And you've wasted a gallon of petrol and several hours of your time to tell me that!'

My mother was unaware of the furore going on around her. A great silence had descended; she seldom spoke unless spoken to. Sitting with a benign smile on her face, she

162

had escaped to a place where there were no more calls on her time. She always knew who her few visitors were and greeted them with the same placid blankness. She exhibited all the signs of the stoicism with which she had ever faced life but the bright intelligence had faded and would never return.

Seventeen

I was reasonably contented with my home life but I still wanted to leave Amy Johnson High School. I answered an advertisement for a job at Ruskin College thinking I was just the sort of person they would want – working-class credentials and creditable academic qualifications – heard nothing for ages and then received a rejection. Philip (who had offered to be my referee) put me straight about such lofty aspirations.

105 Newland Park.
11th November, 1974.

Dear Jean,

I'm sorry – I did get the letter, and thought silence would mean assent. It was good of you to notify me. I've not heard anything from them, though. Oxford is not a very good bet really: everyone wants to get there, and will work 96 hours a week for sod-all to do so. Stick to Salford, Aston, Tower Hamlets!

I don't think I'd really grasped that Alison had gone to Stirling – how grand you must feel with two daughters at university. Laurien must be in her last year?

I'm all right, except that I fell down a flight of steps a few weeks ago and sprained or bruised my arms – can't unscrew bottles & similar essential operations! Still, I can write, as you see.

The world's whole sap is sunk, never mind the garden! I feel cheese dorf.

164

Love as ever,

Philip.

The 'Nocturnal upon St. Lucies Day' reference alludes to an observation in my letter to him, that one of the consolations of November is that the garden can no longer tyrannise since the sap has sunk back to the root.

When Philip found that he could no longer write poems it caused him great anguish. The teasing out of the original idea, the 'given' part of a poem, had invariably been a slow process, usually involving him in much craftsmanship, consulting of dictionaries, and, sometimes, reference to specialists for verification of particular words or phrases he wanted to use. It is too simple to suggest that the upheaval of moving house changed the orderly writing habits of a lifetime, and I am sure the reasons were far more complex than that, but the flight of the muse seemed to coincide with Philip's move to Newland Park and his new status of house owner. He took the responsibility very seriously, having already thought of all the pitfalls, and he worried deeply about them. 'Just move in and run it down,' was my flippant suggestion. Having bought, on a shoestring, our decaying Victorian monster, kept it in reasonable nick, and weathered innumerable disasters such as the ceiling descending on to our spaghetti-filled plates during a dinner party, I could not understand why he should be overawed at the prospect of managing what he described as a one-roomed house. But of course he was a perfectionist and a stickler for quality. Coming from a middle-class background with rigid traditions, he did not enjoy bargain hunting or relish the delights of the tat-shop find (lines 15-17 of his poem, 'Here', make me cringe with self-recognition), so it would all be hideously expensive. Because he liked to be independent, the condition of the garden weighed heavily on his mind and he worried about having to employ someone to tend it. My friend Margot, a neighbour of his, told me she sometimes saw Philip mowing the lawn in his braces, wearing a four-corner knotted hand-kerchief on his head. A card from Philip dated 21st October 1975, reveals his habitual xenophobia, and his paranoia over the garden:

105 Newland Park, Hull.

Dear Jean,

Congratulations on your new job. It came as a sur-prise, as no one had asked me for a reference. You are lucky to get out of school teaching alive by all accounts. What's remedial English? It's a phrase I know, but never really attached a meaning to. Perhaps it's not ending sentences with a preposition.

My new telephone number is –. I'm glad if the tele-phone people are fending off Goole Poetry Workshop and all that. I've got no news: life goes on exactly as before, except that for a few delirious months I had a gardener and have now lost him. Do you know any-thing about weed killer? It seems the only alternative. For the garden, I mean.

Glad the girls are flourishing. Who's Pascal? You don't mean the writer, I suppose. Your experience is probably better than that of a lady I know whose Italy-besotted daughter brought home a string of wops each randier than the last, most of whom tried to sleep with her too. Trials of parenthood! Remember me to them – the girls, I mean.

Your card was delightful – many thanks.

Much love,

Philip.

His choice of greeting-cards vacillated between the anthro-pomorphic and the heavily romantic. He seemed to favour either flopsy bunnies and cute robins or sombre Atkinson Grimshaws and pre-Raphaelite ladies in flowing drapes.

I wonder how far Philip's hatred of 'abroad', and all things foreign, stemmed from early self-consciousness

166

about his speech impediment, allied to a conviction that language is the most important medium of human intercourse. (He loved watching cricket and boxing but seemed to have no desire to express his own physicality.) Not long after we met, he showed me and George photographs of himself as an adolescent on holiday in Germany with his parents. The mood of this viewing was elegiac since Philip was anxious to give proof of his once-luxuriant head of hair. And so we paid due homage to his hirsute youth – long bodied, short-legged and clad in swimming trunks. It occurred to me then that it would have been humiliating for him to struggle with a foreign language whilst trying to keep the stammers at bay. Much of the time he must have felt completely gagged during what were supposed to be enjoyable and broadening continental expeditions.

I had at last found a job in further education, but starting work at the Hull Technical College was a shock to my system. I had just about got the hang of things at the Amy Johnson school by the time I left there but this establishment was quite different. There were wonderful freedoms, such as not being governed by bells, but what I had not realized was that you went to the work rather than have the work come to you. So began twelve years at the chalk-face, humping a heavy bag stuffed with books and folders to two or three decrepit annexes a day. Sometimes I would be timetabled to start a class at one end of the town at the precise time I finished the previous class at the other end. Since I like to be punctual, for the first five years I ran these distances, eating a meat-pie at the gallop, but age and advancing cynicism have slowed me down to a moderate stride. Have you ever seen a Principal run? The main freedom offered to you as Lecturer 1 in a further education college is that of killing yourself from overwork.

I thought the Technical College had hired me to teach remedial English and, indeed, for four hours of the twenty-two-hour week I was required to do that. But my timetable revealed a mass of mystifying abbreviations:

Fab.Weld.1, Gen.Cat.2, Carps.Join.3 and Hair 1, with Gen.Studs. as the subject to be taught for the eighteen remaining hours. Unlike the college Tom Sharpe's Wilt worked at, we had no sewerage workers so Shit 1, 2 and 3 were off the menu but we had most other trades including General, Medical and Intensive Sex, but they turned out to be groups of specialist secretaries. My stock of general knowledge is minuscule so I was horrified when I asked my new boss, a classics scholar, to explain General Studies to me and he replied with a casual dismissive wave of the hand: 'It can be as broad as you want to make it. Balance of Payments, the make-up of political organizations, monetary systems, the history of the Trade Union movement – that kind of thing – oh, and they would find an outline of the tax system useful. But, to get back to the ancient Greeks, their plots are so symmetrical, so perfectly resolved . . .' I had a terrible weekend worrying about how I could quickly become the sort of polymath obviously required, but the reality was much less frightening than the prospect. Most of the classes, apart from the O.N.D. ones, were composed of poorly educated young apprentices who certainly needed some liberal influence in their lives, and I did try to supply it. Using whatever I was currently reading, I floundered through accounts of the barefoot doctors in China, gave them a potted history of the derivation of the English language and outlined the benefits of yoga and healthy eating. I once gave a detailed condemnation of battery-farming to a class of caterers, most of whom subsequently revealed themselves to be the sons and daughters of farmers lucratively engaged in doing just that. I got no converts there. Eventually I realized that their greater need was to learn how to spell, punctuate, and write reports and letters.

Liberal and General Studies departments, which were forced by statute on the old Technical Colleges, were, and still are, the Cinderellas of Further Education. We had no books or materials, only an old Banda machine which

168

tended to chew up your painstakingly typed master copy and spit it out in shards at the other end. You were given a stick of chalk and expected to rely on native wit. A further handicap was the attitude of the majority of the instructors in the technical departments we serviced, who often encouraged their students to believe that general studies was a waste of time and that the lecturers who taught the subject were scruffy Commies obsessed with politics and sex (any sociological topic we discussed was deemed to be dangerous).

Not long after my arrival there, however, a reorganization took place in which all the different sixteen-plus education establishments were gathered together and divided into two large units – Higher Education and Further Education. Our department merged with the College of Commerce and, suddenly, the specialists among us were given large, comforting dollops of GCE work in our particular subject area. This was just what I had wanted but there were drawbacks. Working conditions deteriorated. Higher Education naturally snaffled the better buildings and we were left trying to teach academic subjects in squalid and noisy old annexes. Imagine attempting to analyse a G. M. Hopkins poem in a big, cold room with an 18-foot-high ceiling, Northern Dairies lorries rumbling past the windows and a sheet metal-work class banging away in the room below.

Putting these difficulties aside, though, the work offers great satisfaction. There is nothing quite like teaching literature to groups of people who are hungry to learn, and the part-time classes are mainly composed of such people. Ranging from seventeen years to seventy, they are mostly there on a year's crammer course to qualify themselves for colleges, polytechnics and universities, but some of the older students come simply for a day out and the pleasure of reading and discussing the texts. I asked Beryl, a spry, middle-aged looking woman who had made good progress with her essays and was now getting B's, 'Are you

169

hoping to go to university next year?' 'Oh no,' she said, 'I'm seventy-four, you know. I'd just like to get my Literature A level before I die.' There is no lack of enthusiasm. My main worry was that some of my old-age pensioners might die of hypothermia in the sub-zero temperatures of Park Street Annexe.

Very occasionally there was a discipline problem. Three good-looking, spike-haired boys joined up one year and sat together at the back of the class. It was a big class – about twenty-five – and the room's acoustics were rotten, so it did not help when the trio took to muttering, nudging each other and smirking and tittering at intervals, particularly when I asked, or some member of the class answered, a question. I tried to make them join in but they were far too laid back to do that. One day, when I was angry enough to burst, I waylaid them outside the room and asked for an explanation: did they not like the subject, perhaps economics was more in their line, what was so funny, and so forth. They were silent. 'What's wrong with you, anyway?' I asked in desperation. The tallest one considered this for a moment and said 'I'm immature.' Repressing the twin desire to a) hit him and b) laugh, I said, 'Well sod off and be immature in somebody else's class if you can't behave decently in mine.' They put in a couple more appearances for pride's sake and then, mercifully, faded away.

The other half of my teaching timetable was with a class called the Pre-TOPS (Training Opportunities), a Manpower Services Commission sponsored course which originally had an intake of fifteen people aged eighteen years and over. They attended full-time for a year and the purpose of the course was to improve their English and maths to make them more employable. We attracted a good sprinkling of housewives in their late twenties and mid-thirties, whose children were growing up and who wanted to be able to aim higher than the Metal Box or Bird's Eye factories. There were men who had done a succession of dead-end labouring jobs and whose instincts told them they could aspire to more congenial work if only they knew the difference between *there* and *their*, and we invariably had a couple of foreigners who needed to be able to read and write English. Our brief from the MSC was to make these people sufficiently literate and numerate to get through a narrow set of trade tests, from whence they could go on TOPS courses and become plumbers, typists, caterers, etc. We complied, of course, but we had bigger ideas for them. For Ann Jackson, Frank Redpath and me, this course became our crusade and we gave it everything we had.

Subversively (MSC thought it would give them ideas above their station when we tentatively suggested it), I took them through a Mode 3 O-level English-language course that, to their astonishment and delight, 95% of them passed. We subsequently steered the more gifted ones on to our own A-level courses, the better to supervise and sustain them, and encouraged them to apply to universities. The ones who took the leap were all married people with dependent children, so this step required great sacrifices of them and their families. We soon had three graduates, and others in the pipeline, not to mention those who made less outwardly impressive but equally significant strides. Our main tenet was that competition with others is destructive and that if you have improved your own performance then you have succeeded. Our intake was truly comprehensive and each year the students were of very mixed ability, from those who could scarcely read or write to the uneducated, but naturally-gifted, ones.

Some years there were explosive mixtures of character and personality and there was never a time when there were no headaches. It was always difficult to be detached and not let their worries dominate your private life. I found myself lying awake at nights trying to solve their mostly insoluble problems: Should we persuade Ginny to try Marriage Guidance? Would it be wrong to suggest the possibility of abortion to Debra? Could I afford to lend

James and Karen their exam fees? What sort of exercises could I devise to show Raj the difference between p and b? One afternoon, Derek, a big, bluff Irishman, who had been to the pub at lunchtime to give himself courage, came into the class late and announced that he had something to say. The class looked up from their Stan Barstow book and gave him their attention. 'I want to tell you . . . I feel you ought to know . . . that I'm bisexual', he brought out, with a mixture of pride, shame and defiance. The custodian of all their secrets, I looked round the impassive faces of the class, which included a trade unionist exile from Chile, a pioneering lesbian feminist, a one-time pimp, an almost-reformed alcoholic, a refugee from the lower ranks of the London underworld, and a young woman whose body daily bore testimony to fresh non-accidental injuries inflicted by her father. Derek, waiting in vain for shocked gasps of 'Ooh' and 'Ah', quietly subsided into his fairisle pullover when they yawned, turned back to their books and said, 'We're on page 63.'

Everyone who taught on this course became deeply committed to it and felt it was a noble enterprise that should be expanded and developed. Sadly, though, the funding authorities whittled away at it and cut the staying time of the students down to fifteen, twelve or six weeks, depending on their ability, so that only the most remedial were with us for the full fifteen weeks. The administrators were delighted with the new system for, over the year, the course processed far greater numbers and the balance sheet looked more impressive. We felt we had ceased being educators and had become conveyor-belt operators. Nevertheless, even students from the etiolated courses stop us in the street and say, 'Thank you for changing my life'. Gratifying though this is, we know we could have done so much more given a sane education policy. At Easter 1986 the MSC withdrew its funding and the course closed.

Eighteen

Marine Eng. II were the *crème de la crème* of the Technical College and they knew it. They were paid £30 a week, on top of their digs allowance, by the shipping companies which employed them, so they were well-off by most students' standards – and by mine. When I entered the classroom, they would crackle Coke cans and shuffle playing-cards for a token two minutes, not to appear too uncool, then they would settle down to listen. After a few weeks I noticed a six foot, flaxen-haired Billy Budd of a lad who asked lots of questions in a curious East Anglian accent, and was eager to learn. When we met unexpectedly in a local pub, we discovered that we were neighbours and, wasting no time, he asked me if I would help him précis eight hundred words down to three hundred for some technical piece he was writing. Never having been one to deny a student assistance, I hacked the work down to the required length and he invited me out to a sumptuous dinner by way of thanks. From then on he haunted my house, calling in to see if I needed any odd jobs doing, asking me out for drinks or walks to the pier, or to look at barges and other craft on the river Hull. He took on the job of feeding Loki and Pesk, the two cats I had inherited from Alison, when I went away for weekends, and cooked delicious meals for me when I returned. I was somewhat guarded at first, feeling that he was too good to be true but, after a few months, I welcomed his unequivocal friendliness. At the same time, I saw that, to an outsider, it must seem a rum business. After all, he was twenty-five years younger than I and we had very little in common apart from a shared interest in food and making each other laugh. I was charmed by the novelty of being deferred to and found I enjoyed being the one to decide and whose opinions were valued.

One day he asked if I should like to go to Haworth. It was the end of July 1976 and college had finished. In a week's time Peter was due to join his ship for six months' sea service. We spent an idyllic day walking to the Brontë waterfalls, getting soaked in the frequent heavy rain showers, drying out in the baking sun, and eating handfuls of bilberries. Going towards the station, on the way back, I made some remark about how astonishing it was to think of Charlotte, Emily and Co. walking on those same cobbles. Peter looked bewildered and so I enlarged a bit: 'You know. The Brontës.' 'Who are they?' he asked. 'The famous family of writers who used to live here', I hinted heavily. 'Isn't that why you wanted to come here?' 'No', he answered, unabashed, 'I came for the railway.' 'What's special about that?' I asked. 'It's the famous Keighley-Worth Valley Railway', he answered, appalled by my ignorance. During the twelve years we have lived together we have suffered many more similar culture shocks.

Before he embarked on the B.P. tanker *British Hazel*, Peter told me that he loved me and asked if I would write to him. So I wrote once a week, as I had written to Laurien when she was at Château-du-Loire and as I did for two years to Ali in Botswana. I am a lazy correspondent but I know how important to the exile regular letters from home can be. At Sutton House we belted through the morning's scrubbings and polishings, willing the bell to ring for cocoa time when there would be a stampede to the kitchen. Twenty or so expectant girls clustered round Matron, who stood at the table dispensing the mail, and often there would be tears if the hoped-for letter did not arrive.

I had fallen in love with Peter three days before he left Hull. We were wandering round the garden one evening sniffing the golden honeysuckle, admiring the drifts of pink bush roses, sprinklings of purple-spotted foxgloves, the spiky red-hot pokers, the army of teasels and a forest of shirley poppies I had allowed to seed. Unlike Philip, I find gardening no problem. I like herbs and semi-wild plants that come up annually so, apart from doing swops with other gardeners, and bits of weeding and cutting back, I let it go its own way. 'One of these years,' I said to Peter, as we sipped glasses of wine, 'I'll save up and have that air-raid shelter demolished.' It stood there, an ugly brick blot with a fifteen-inch-thick concrete roof, a few yards away from the house, casting murk, mould and bad vibes all round itself. 'Have you got a sledge hammer?' he asked. 'Yes, I think Warren and Anne left one. Why?' 'I'll get up early tomorrow morning and do it for you', he replied. And he did. A telephone call brought his classmate, a muscular, crew-cut boy called Ian Flood, round with a bag of his dad's tools. Dressed only in vests, jeans and plimsolls, with no protective gear, they bashed away in the broiling sun for two days and it was down. It cost me quids in lemonade, beer and square meals for the workers. After Peter and Ian departed, Laurien, Alison, her friend Chris, sundry small boys and I barrowed bricks and rubble non-stop into two hired skips and within the week we had our first glorious and unimpeded view of the whole garden. A man who will knock your shelter down, I thought, is a man worth loving.

Six months later, when his sea service finished, Peter arrived on the doorstep with his bag, a bottle of cointreau and some choice presents purchased in Sicily and at various ports of call in the Arctic Circle. I thought he had perhaps just come for a few days holiday but after several months I realized that he had moved in. My friends accepted him and the great disparity in our ages without comment (to our faces, anyway). He had learned how to cook rich,

175

aromatic dishes by watching the Indian crew on the tanker and he soon became the Head Serang in my kitchen, knocking up scrumptious meals and copious batches of bread for the extended family.

Laurien, back from Newcastle University and a teaching certificate in York, was teaching French in a local school and living at home. Alison and Chris, a pre-Raphaelite-looking youth, were having their statutory year off from the Human Purposes and Communication degree course at Bradford University. This sabbatical was designed for students to find purposeful jobs and gain industrial experience, but there were not many jobs going that year, purposeful or otherwise. The great unemployment bulge was beginning to be felt and Peter, Chris and Ali were incredulous when they received no replies to their many letters of application. They were not aiming high but even the most grotty jobs were over-subscribed.

Communal life was not all roses, of course. There were plenty of personality clashes and much fratching. I tried to make allowances for their various frustrations and smooth things over but one weekend I thought, damn the lot of them, and escaped to the clear air of Joyce and Steve's at Westcliff-on-Sea. Their adult company and good advice is always restorative. When I arrived back at Hull Paragon Station, Peter met me at the barrier, his face pale with strain, 'Thank God you've come back.'

After a couple of months searching, he found work with British Rail at the Priory Sidings Depot as a carriage and wagon repairer – heavy hammer stuff that left him stunned and weary at the end of a day that began at 7.30 a.m. His clothes and flesh were regularly punctured with burn-holes from the awkward welding operations he had to perform, but he loved the camaraderie he felt being with five middle-aged men, skilled at their jobs, and each one of them a repository of knowledge about life, the last war and the industrial processes they had seen come and go. Peter was impressed by the trust and care they all showed in carrying out their dangerous teamwork, where one slip of the hammer or a moment's inattention can mean a man's hand is lost or a foot crushed.

Coming from a well-regulated household, Peter had to make a number of adjustments to mine. When laying the table for our first non-family dinner party, he looked scathingly at the assortment of plain, flowered or willow-patterned crockery and the junk-shop miscellany of knives and forks, and asked, 'Where do you keep your matching plates and cutlery?'

A couple of years later, I telephoned to invite Philip to dinner and to introduce him to Peter. How was I to tell someone as conventional as Philip that I was living with a man so much younger than I? I did it embarrassedly and in a rush: 'He's very nice; he's not literary, he works for the railway and he's interested in steam.' Philip did his home-work and came prepared to talk to Peter about a distant Larkin relative who had worked for the railways and writ-ten a book about them. Seeing Peter's size, however, he realized they had a closer bond and said, 'You must have problems buying clothes to fit.' For the next half hour they talked about the difficulty of finding shirts that didn't garotte them at the neck and leap out of their trousers at the bottom end. Philip recommended Mr High and Mighty. Peter recommended Oxfam. At dinner Philip said he would have only one of the profiteroles Peter had made but in fact he ate three. After the meal he fell asleep briefly and was very apologetic. 'I seem to do this all the time', he said. He complained about the rising price of laundry services. This seemed to me a terribly archaic way of get-ting clothes clean. 'Haven't you a washing machine?' I asked. 'Good God, no, but I wash my own socks and underclothes out. It gives me quite a lot of pleasure in fact. Very satisfying dabbling and wringing and then seeing them hang out to dry.' This arose from my comment that he no longer wore gaudy socks. I had always thought of them as the leavening feature of his otherwise sober

177

appearance – they were usually petunia or vermilion. 'They've all turned the same colour in the wash', he said regretfully.

I asked him if he had a new book ready. Roughly the desired number of years he needed to hatch one seemed to have elapsed. 'Well, you know how I usually have half a dozen substantial ones and eighteen or so fillers?' I nodded. 'I've got the fillers', he said, taking another gulp of water and gazing wanly out of the window.

Once you know and love a person, beauty or the lack of it seem irrelevant since the face is the register of a person's qualities. Philip's face was so mobile and expressive of his feelings that I could not understand his frequent complaints about his receding chin and his big nose. When I told him they did not detract from his charm, he gave his satyr's leer. I did sympathize with him over his baldness; he had been so young when fate played that nasty trick on him. When he was animated and clowning about, his face was boyish and had a real sweetness but his sardonic, savage look, if he was angry about something, pulled all the planes down into jowly flaps. Misery did that too.

He always felt (who does not?) that the *next* photograph would show his face transformed into the one he really wanted. When he first acquired his camera he would focus it, set the timer, then rush round to his seat and pose, hoping to produce a more handsome image than hitherto. When Humphrey Ocean was painting his portrait I asked Philip how it was going. The glum look took over as he said that at first he had been rather taken with it – it made him look like the young Mussolini – but after several hours more work it looked like Hitchcock at eighty.

Marion Shaw, a lecturer in the English Department and, from its inception, a staunch supporter of the Marvell Press, invited me to a poetry reading to be given at the University Library on 1 November 1984. Philip, looking very bulky round the middle, gave a witty and charming introduction and endpiece. It struck me that he would have made an excellent jazz club compère. Introducing Blake Morrison, poetry editor of *The Observer*, and Andrew Motion, poetry editor of Chatto & Windus, he said how awed he felt to be in the presence of two such powerful young men: – 'Andrew can actually stop you getting your book published. But if it is published, Blake can make sure it gets slammed.' Every line he spoke contained drollery of some kind. While the poets were reading, he sat at the side wearing his Cheshire-cat face. It sagged a bit during the long poems.

Afterwards, at Marion's house, he was very sociable and seemed relaxed although I noticed, with some surprise, that whilst we were talking he smoked a number of cigarettes. He had always struck me as a very moderate smoker. I asked after Monica. He said she was still ill and that he was taking her to see a specialist at nine o'clock the following morning, which was why he could not stay long. He asked after our mutual friend, Ted Tarling, saying that he kept Ted's painting of Stoneferry in his kitchen where he could see it most often. He was most anxious that I should understand his reason for choosing the kitchen as a setting for the picture. I told him Ted was feeling dizzy and he said that he also suffered from dizziness. I put it down to his being overweight at which he pulled a face. He said that George had written to announce the birth of a son but he had not replied in case they asked him to be godfather. He went on, 'And he sent me a photograph of a baby! It's like sending garlic to Dracula.' I said something about George not being good at keeping up friendships, to which Philip replied that he himself was not much good at that. He pulled a gloomy face and said it was *The Less Deceived* accounts time, which always made him nervous. Would he get the money on time or wouldn't he? If it came too late he couldn't include it in his tax return.

Philip said that he would dearly love to see a selected or collected poems published since he was not likely to write any more verse but that, despite very good offers from

179

Faber, George refused to allow them to make any selections from *The Less Deceived*. He enquired solicitously after the back-end of my house which was, owing to subsidence, parting company with the main structure. He was particularly keen to know if the insurance company would fork out for the rebuilding since he too was having problems with his house: disturbing cracks had appeared in the walls. He mentioned retirement and said how much he was dreading it. Then he told an Irish joke that he had heard told on the telly, after the snooker: 'Mother, I'm pregnant'. Reply: 'Are you sure it's yours?' Every time he saw me he told me a joke, but I usually forgot them.

A few months before this meeting, I had a long telephone conversation with Philip. My life at that time contained rather more emotional convolutions than usual and, led on by his sympathetic interest, I confided to him more of the tangled web than I normally would have. Coming breathlessly to an end, I waited for his response. There was an extremely long pause during which I thought I had, perhaps, bored him into a coma, or offended his sense of what could decently be told by one friend to another. When he did speak, I was surprised by the wistfulness of his tone: 'You've always had such an exciting life, Jean. You've always done what you wanted and had the courage to take chances.'

My initial reaction was to wonder how a man who seemed to be so successful and secure, could possibly envy my constrained yet rather rackety life and modest achievements. But, of course, we had been talking of romantic involvement and in such matters, as so many of his poems reveal, what Philip might gain by plunging in had always been carefully weighed against what he stood to lose. It saddened me to hear him voice his regret at having invariably allowed his head to rule his heart.

Nineteen

In 1970, I was in my second year at Hull University when Ted Tarling, who had for years earned a modest living as a semi-professional jazz musician, told me he wanted to engage in literary activity. Unable to find a little magazine to his liking, he decided to publish his own and asked me to help with it. I was tied up with Defoe, Pope and Longinus, but I agreed to be his business manager and give him a hand to get started. He chose the name The Sonus Press for his imprint.

After he had obtained one or two estimates from printers, he realized that this method of production was beyond his means and asked George if he thought it would be possible to edit, print and publish a magazine of one's own. George said it would not; there would be far too much work. When Ted's sister, Barbara, bought him a hand-worked Adana Eight-Five platen press and some type be took up the challenge, bought himself a primer on printing for the amateur – John Ryder's *Printing for Pleasure* – and got on with printing the sheaf of poems he had already, somewhat presumptuously, solicited.

A month later, after much expense and hard labour (in cold weather he still feels a pain in his left shoulder from all that handle cranking), the first issue of *Wave* was out. When asked by an American professor, who was compiling an encyclopedia of British literary magazines, to give some information about the genesis of *Wave*, Ted replied, 'For me, publishing a poetry magazine was like heaving a brick over a high wall.'

Tastefully presented, workmanlike and giving every appearance of their printer having been apprentice-trained, *Wave*'s thirty-two pages contained poems by Joan Barton, Thomas Blackburn, Alan Brownjohn, Bob Cobbing, Eugen Gomringer, Michael Hamburger, Elizabeth Jennings, Philip Larkin, Laurence Lerner, Edwin Morgan, Norman Nicholson, Peter Porter, Peter Redgrove, Vernon Scannell, R. S. Thomas, Anthony Thwaite and Ted Walker. It was not reviewed. Joan Barton, who had been a friend of John Betjeman for many years, passed on Betjeman's comment that *Wave* was the best of its kind he had seen for years. Ted used this comment in *Wave*'s advertising blurb. Ted's broad editorial policy was to publish poems which possessed clarity and which said something interesting or moving in a competent manner.

Philip was living in Oxford at this time and compiling his *Oxford Book of Twentieth-Century English Verse*. He had promised Ted a poem for the first issue but pressure to complete his anthology was heavy and by the middle of September, when Ted had printed the entire magazine apart from page 32, Philip's poem had not arrived. Just in time and apologizing for the delay, Philip posted his poem 'How' to Ted on the 21st September. Ted set it up and printed it the same day. The following day he stapled the pages of the magazine together and sent off the complimentary copies. Philip received his copies, complete with his poem, on the 23rd September along with a note saying, 'Is this a record?' to which Philip replied, 'More than a record – a miracle'.

The magazine ran for eight issues and among the interesting newcomers it introduced were Anne Stevenson, Valerie Owen and Frank Redpath. Ted had seen some of Joan Barton's poems in *Listen* and had liked them very much. He asked her to contribute to the first issue of *Wave*. Joan's poems are lucid and sensuous, rooted in the places she has known and loved. Closer acquaintance with her work convinced Ted that he should produce a collection of it and he wrote to her asking if she was prepared to submit such a collection. Joan, who was born in 1908, responded with a heap of manuscript, the earliest poem dated 1928. In 1972, she and her friend Barbara Watson were running a bookselling business in Salisbury. Prior to this, they had for many years managed The White Horse Bookshop in Marlborough. Joan's letters were full of fascinating detail about bookselling on a shoestring, including the following anecdote:

> . . . My life has been very dull comparably, though some of our early struggles almost match up. In the first few weeks we procured with great labour a copy of Rupert Brooke's poems, then out of print, for a farm labourer's wife in a nearby village (very cultured in these parts, we thought) and she actually paid for it before disclosing that she had really wanted a RUPERT BOOK.

During the Second World War, Joan had been the director of a department at the British Council. John Betjeman was a member of her staff and she showed Ted a letter John had sent her in 1945 commenting on her earlier work:

> You are a lovely poet. Make no doubt of it. Reading your poems all through the rain this morning I am moved beyond words by some passages in Nether Stowey which I have marked in pencil . . . You really should publish them in book form – not leave them in magazines. I would suggest Macmillans although I know no one there, and I fancy the title of the MSS should be Bristol and Somerset because these are the atmospheres which surround them and the names would give significance to the reader of the poems who knew the places.

Encouraged by having his own assessment of Joan's work confirmed, Ted showed the manuscript to Philip who took it away with him to Scotland that summer of 1971. Philip was less than enthusiastic, as his letter of 7 August shows: 'It might, I suppose be possible to build a book around these [the poems Philip had suggested] but it would have to be a selection and, as you say, with an introduction by Betjeman.' Undaunted by a shortage of money, Philip's reservations, and Betjeman's subsequent reluctance to write an introduction, Ted set to work. Through the good offices of Eric Walter White he received an Arts Council grant of £300 to print this book and two others, though half this amount was swallowed up by the binder's bill and the rest was spent on paper and type.

In the small 'press room' of his mother's house in East Hull, Ted did the printing and co-ordinated all the processes necessary to the launching of this very creditable slim volume of poems. When *The Mistress and Other Poems* came out in April 1972, Betjeman wrote to Joan:

I don't think you know how beautiful your poems are. I am more pleased to have them than I can say. Not a word wasted. Of course I should not write an introduction. They need none. They speak for themselves and they inspire me. I have sent a copy to David Cecil who much likes them. You do not have to be a Cliftonian to appreciate their worth – nor an East Anglian. They are poetry. Love to Barbara. Yours, John Betjeman.

Philip too was complimentary:

32 Pearson Park
21 April, 1972

Dear Ted,

It was a delightful surprise to find *The Mistress* downstairs tonight – had you rung the bell? I'm so deaf I never hear it. I'd been thinking about it and wondering how it was progressing.

The production seems very good to me, considering

the difficulties you work under. Good t/p, lovely jacket, and a layout coping successfully with her long lines. I don't really care for the square brackets round the page numbers, and surely the stuff on the verso of the ½ title ought to be on the verso of the title? And is this sticky tape necessary?

Reading the poems makes me wonder if I was less than fair to them. They do sprawl and lack concision, but most have heart, which after all is a *sine qua non*. I hope they get good reviews. Will you send many review copies out?

Anyway, I'd like 5 copies, cheque enclosed. Leave them in at the Library some time.

Do send to Eric White's successor as Literature Director, Charles Osborne, at the Arts Council.

My life has been rather upset since January when my mother fell and has seemed to fail a little in consequence – she's in a nursing home and I've been going to see her at weekends, near Leicester. Hence life has had to be crammed into 5 days a week, and been depressed and worried in consequence.

However, the purpose of this letter is to congratulate you on producing an individual contribution to the poetry of our time. The book is like the poems – a sincere and personal labour of love, and does you great honour.

Yours sincerely, Philip.

Later that year Betjeman was made Poet Laureate and Philip comments on the Laureateship in his next letter to Ted, dated 20 October 1972.

. . . I was oddly surprised at Betjeman getting the L'ship: I thought he might be thought a bit old. But I'm very glad. Glad it's over too: it was rather a dreadful period, like being in an audience at a pantomime when the comedian was picking on members of the audience, even though I was confident I shouldn't be in their minds *really*.

In 1973 *The Oxford Book of Twentieth-Century English Verse* was published. That this was the culmination of herculean scholarship on Philip's part is made plain in Anthony Thwaite's radio interview which was broadcast by the BBC soon after its appearance – Philip read the whole of twentieth century published poetry and simply chose from the lot. The last thing shoestring publishers can afford is the kind of advertising for which they have to pay. They are therefore dependent on free publicity and it is vital that when references are made, or quotations appear, they are accompanied by the name and address of the Press. Without this it is virtually impossible for the would-be buyer to ferret out the source of the publication. Philip had included in the anthology the title poem from Joan's book *The Mistress*, and when he realized that the publishers had failed to print an acknowledgement to The Sonus Press, he was fully aware of the tragedy.

Leicester, Easter Sunday 1973.

Dear Ted,

I am sorry not to have replied earlier. I seem to be a poor letter-writer these days.

I hadn't noticed there were no acknowledgements to you for the Joan Barton poem – this was a side of things I didn't handle. This is a great disappointment as I had hoped it would make her book better known: please excuse us all. I think the sooner we have a reprint the better, there are so many mistakes. What pleasure I might have had out of it has quite disappeared.

I'm sorry you heard no more about the library post, but I expected your application sounded too unusual for them. Someone ought to rewrite a fable of the ant and the grasshopper, with the latter trying to get a job without any references or previous experience. I wish you could become a good printing firm! I never seem to get a job done without some mistake or other.

Not a very cheerful Easter – visiting my aged mother in a nursing home in the afternoons. A few more years shall roll.

The DHSS was complaining of Ted's prolonged unemployment and was requesting evidence of his applications for jobs. Among the subsequent spoof applications he made was one regarding a Library Assistant post at the Brynmor Jones Library. He concluded this application with, 'I shan't bore you with further details of my working life except to add that, through it all, I chafed to become a Library Assistant. Incidentally, perhaps you might pass on my warmest congratulations to the lovely young lady who will be awarded this particular post.' Philip later told Douglas Dunn that a lovely young lady had indeed been successful.

Time did not hang heavily on Ted's hands, however, as he still played the clarinet and saxophones on the occasional one-night stand, attended to the sales side of The Sonus Press and always had a new issue of *Wave* simmering. After the penultimate issue had been printed and distributed, Philip wrote to Ted:

20th July, 1973

Many thanks for *Wave* 7. Valerie Owen is certainly interesting, and I found J. Barton moving, though did she really write 'chum' in the last verse? I don't get it. Seems to jar.

No news I'm afraid. It seems a long time since I wrote anything. Winter silence closes in, light the lamp and pour the gin. Oh dear!

Philip.

This seems an unseasonal couplet for mid-summer, but Philip always looked ahead. His first paragraph refers to

Joan Barton's poem, 'The Major: An Epitaph', in which she tells of how she once went to a private house book sale, sat at the Major's desk, and was able to imagine the sad pattern of his life through looking at his books and old diaries. She asked the reader, 'Why after twenty years should I still care?/Not out of pity, chum, nor love . . .' Ted conveyed to Joan Philip's misgivings over the word 'chum' and she readily substituted 'now'.

Philip and Ted were both devoted lovers of jazz. Unfortunately, Philip's love stopped at bebop whereas Ted's taste was more eclectic and his own playing showed a marked preference for post-Parker music. Despite this basic gulf, they found much common ground and they even shared musical evenings. One impromptu duet took place at Douglas Dunn's house with Ted playing Dougie's clarinet. He incorporated plenty of Charlie Parker 'licks' into the blues number in order to taunt Philip who provided a rhythm section accompaniment using Lesley Dunn's knitting needles and the *Radio Times*. Ten years later he referred to this incident in a letter to Ted (17 January 1984): 'I should love to hear you play again, even with those modern embellishments that you kindly warned me of before producing them.' Stung by Philip's frequent attacks on Charlie Parker, Ted was provoked into writing a defensive limerick:

> The saxophone playing of Bird,
> Was quite, claimed a poet, absurd.
>   Had not the young bopper
>   Erewhile come a cropper
> He might have played on undeterred.

He followed it up with a clerihew which showed his admiration for Parker's innovatory music:

> Bebop stars
> Drove similar cars

But Bird's horn went *bibid*
And the others went *ibid*.

By 1974 Ted had printed and published *The Mistress* and eight issues of *Wave*. Looking at the last two issues I am still impressed by the highly professional production and chaste format of the magazine. Ted not only provided a platform for new poets, many of whom subsequently made a reputation for themselves, but he also represented the work of established writers such as Elizabeth Jennings, Martin Seymour-Smith, Peter Porter, John Lehmann, William Plomer, Douglas Dunn, Alan Sillitoe, P. J. Kavanagh, John Wain, Vernon Scannell, Philip Hobsbaum, Laurence Lerner and John Holloway. But his four years of publishing experience had taught him that marketing poetry would never be anything other than a too-expensive hobby. Ted had discovered, as had George and I before him, that the only satisfaction to be gained from this kind of work is that of feeling the job has been well done. Without the capital necessary to advertise and build up a distribution network, your editions, and therefore your sales, will be small and the profit non-existent. The only bonus such activity brings you is a wide circle of pen-pals; this too can cost a fortune in postage stamps.

In a spirit of parochialism, for he knew that a private or an American sale would have been more lucrative, Ted offered to sell the *Wave* archive to the Brynmor Jones Library. Philip replied on the 17th May 1974:

Thank you for offering us this archive, which the archivist and I have looked at with interest.

I am prepared to offer £100 for the material you deposited with us, on condition that I can secure a 25% subvention for the purpose from the Arts Council. Perhaps you will let me know whether this offer is acceptable to you, in which case I will write to the

Literature Director to see whether he thinks his funds might be made available for such a purpose.

Ted accepted the modest sum and handed over his files.

In January 1977 Ted moved the press and his belongings into an attic flat just off Pearson Park from where Philip had recently moved. Shortly after, a new tenant, who worked at Hull University when he wasn't working at home, moved into the flat below him. He was attempting to perfect a machine which, as far as Ted could make out, would enable one to tune into one's own dreams. Seeing his head festooned with an elaborate spaghetti junction of wires, Baron Frankenstein would have recognized a friend and colleague. Ted was moved to parody:

> *Nights*
> What are nights for?
> Nights are where we sleep.
>
> They come, they numb us
> Time and time over.
> They are to be dreamed in:
> Where can we dream but sleep?
>
> Ah, solving that question
> Brings Dr Keith Hearne
> With his bloody machine
> Patented over the world.

In 1983 Ted started up the press again to print and publish *The Wild Whistle*, a collection of songs he had written in the traditional idiom along with his own versions of some traditional songs. The printing of the music had been a laborious and tricky job. Ted drew by hand a master copy and took it to a local printer who reproduced it by the offset litho process. The same firm made a hash of the trimming of a large number of copies and so rendered them unsaleable. When Ted sent a copy of the book to Philip he gave him an account of the mishaps. Philip replied sympathetically on the 9th October 1983 and referred obliquely to *Required Writing* – his own forthcoming publication – which he no doubt felt was a poor substitute for a successor to *High Windows*.

Thank you for sending me The Wild Whistle. The story of its production is hair-raising – can you not get compensation from these wreckers? My copy seems all right to the lay eye. The music is beautifully done – surely it's too accurate to be hand-written, and too expensive to be printed? Is it letraset?

As for the words, I'm not sure how far they're 'localisations' of existing songs (where that's applicable) and how far original but they are simple and moving. I imagine even more so when sung. I'll get one for the library: it will go in the 'H' section (local rarities). What a man of many parts you are!

Yes I am as spritely as ever, which means not bloody spritely at all. For the last six months I've been justifying my existence by looking after a convalescent friend who fell ill at Easter and needed somewhere to be. I have a collection of hack-work coming out next month- ought to be called *Bottom of the Barrel* – which will no doubt earn me a good ballocking in the literary press. People keep talking about retirement, making me feel my age.

No doubt things will cheer up. I'm sorry you're not playing any more; surely anyone who plays as well as you do must miss it, not to mention your audiences. But I hope that the book sells in compensation.

Yrs. ever, Philip

Despite his disclaimer, *Required Writing* is a fine, though by no means complete, collection of Philip's witty and wise reflections on life, literature and music. His interests can be seen to be scholarly and wide-ranging, and many of

191

the literary pieces refute the philistinism of which he has often been accused. His severe limitations are shown by the line he draws at that gang of P's: Parker, Pound, Picasso and Pollock, but in evaluating work that follows traditional lines he is succinct, stimulating and candid. What one does not learn about the essential Philip from his poetry and fiction can be gleaned from this collection. It is a pity he did not include other worthwhile pieces such as the article he wrote in 1970 for the student magazine *Torch*, and the delightful recollection of boyhood – 'Not the Place's Fault' – but no doubt they will be collected at some future date.

On the 17th January Philip wrote to Ted:

. . . My friend Michael Bowen is arranging a concert at the University in May (25th) to commemorate Ellington's death (tenth anniversary): Midnight Follies plus Adelaide Hall! So keep the date open if you are so inclined. A. Hall must be about 90.

. . . I began 1984 with flu, or what they now call virus infection, but am more or less all right.

I hope you survived your Oxford-Cambridge trips: both of them *very cold* places in my experience. Did you find your book in Blackwell's Music Shop? Did you send review copies out? I hope it is making its way.

I am currently inching my way through a vast tome of Evelyn Waugh's reviews etc. with a view to enlightening the Observer's readers about it, so this can't be a long letter. Let's hope 1984 is a good year for us both. For me it has begun with a friend chucking himself under a train at Tufnell Park or somewhere, with fatal results. I'm sure we can avoid that.

Yours ever, Philip.

Ted invited me to go with him to the Midnight Follies concert. We enjoyed the occasion, though the music was

less than stunning, and it was good to see the flam-
boyantly-dressed Adelaide Hall looking chipper and
thoroughly enjoying herself. Although Ted and Philip had
written to each other and talked over the telephone, several
years had passed since they last met. Before the concert
began Philip, who was wearing two hearing aids, spotted
me and came over to chat, all the while casting a suspicious
eye over Ted. After a time it became clear that he did not
recognize Ted who, to use his own denigrating phrase,
had become fat, bald and bearded. Philip puzzled away,
obviously thinking while he kept up the conversational
flow: It's definitely not Peter; it must be a new bloke.
Before I could find a way of enlightening him, the
musicians came on and the concert began. During the
interval in the Middleton Hall's crowded and noisy coffee-
drinking area, Philip and I bellowed pleasantries at each
other and when he moved off to speak to an acquaintance,
I introduced Ted to Monica. I can imagine his mortifica-
tion when Monica later revealed to him my mysterious
companion's identity for it brought forth the following
apology:

26th May, 1984.
I am writing to apologise for my complete failure to
recognise you last night – you must have been taken
aback. When Monica told me 'who Jean was with' I
nearly expired with shame and remorse. You *told* me
you would be there, you *told* me you would ask Jean –
all this had gone from my so-called mind since 29 March
when you last wrote. I really am dreadfully sorry. I suppose it's some years since we saw each other and I may
be forgiven to some extent but oh dear, what an awful
mistake.

I don't know if deaf men should go to jazz concerts; I
had a pretty disjointed impression of the whole thing,
some bits being loud (audible), others (inc. A. Hall) inaudible. This kind of pastiche is nicer to listen to than

original Ornette, but it still is pastiche, don't you think? I bought one of their records in the interval, but don't react any differently. What did you think?

Let me know if you drink lunch: we will arrange one. I haven't said how sorry I am about Joan Barton's blindness. Write when your fury has abated.

Yours, Philip.

Soon after, Philip followed up this letter with a telephone call saying he wished to stand Ted a meal at a restaurant of his choice. Ted, whose life borders on the ascetic and is therefore no connoisseur of splendid eateries, suggested they meet at the Good Fellowship, a mock-Tudor pub situated so close to the University that he imagined it must be Philip's local and therefore convenient for him. Once there, it emerged that Philip had not been inside the place for years. He liked its dimly-lit ambience and said it reminded him of London pubs.

Over lunch, after each had explained to the other that frequent dizzy spells suggested death was imminent, Philip spoke of no longer being able to write poetry. He said he had always wanted to write another novel and when Ted asked him what kind of novel he replied, smiling, that he would like to write about a young nurse who meets a young doctor, a newcomer to the village. Ted asked if Mills and Boon were aware of his plans and he replied that he would like to write a *good* novel but, unfortunately, he was not clever enough to do so and, anyway, good novels did not sell these days.

They spoke of the changing Hull landscape and Ted mentioned that he was trying to paint some of it while there was still time. Philip asked Ted why he didn't take up painting as a career and Ted explained to him the practical problems including those of the poor quality of light in his flat and the lack of space there. He went on to explain his technical problems and Philip offering his left ear, the better one, listened patiently until he had finished. 'Well', he crooned nervously. 'What do you mean, well?' Ted asked. 'I mean I haven't understood a bloody word you've just said', he replied. Philip's old friend, Monica Jones, recently told Ted she thought Philip knew more about painting and pictures than he admitted to knowing. Looking through the 250 or so letters Philip wrote to his artist friend, Jim Sutton, (part of the Larkin archive at Hull's Brynmor Jones Library) one can see his interest in and knowledge of trends in European art. The drawings that accompany most of the letters show Philip to be a decisive and witty cartoonist. Each one illustrates a current activity or state of mind and a collection of these drawings would make an interesting commentary on his early life.

Philip agreed that it was unlikely there would be much money in painting for a living. 'At least', he added, 'writers are tossed a few crumbs while they're still alive to enjoy them.' Ted showed him several snapshots of his most recent paintings and Philip seemed to like them. He sent Ted a note on 15 June 1984:

> It was a pleasure to meet you yesterday, though my spirits sank steadily throughout the rest of the day; I think it must have been the Hull Brewery bitter, never a favourite of mine. I was much impressed by your paintings. There ought to be one in the Ferens Art Gallery.

Philip's preoccupation with his health was as long-standing and well-developed as his fear of death and, indeed, one of our favourite jokes was the question and answer routine from one of Peter de Vries' novels: 'What's the best present you can give a hypochondriac? A bowl of wax fruit.' However, by this time there was no question of his complaints being psychosomatic. He was overweight, he took little exercise and he had suffered a thrombosis.

A couple of months later Ted gave Philip a landscape painting of a view of Stoneferry in return for several kindnesses. I am deeply envious for, although Ted is the soul of generosity, he is not easily parted from his pictures. I have been angling for one for years but with no success. He puts me off with 'No, the shadows are not right', or, 'The varnish went wrong on that one.' The letter of thanks Philip wrote sheds light on his preferences in art – a subject on which I have not seen him express his views elsewhere:

7th August, 1984.

Dear Ted,

I am at a loss to say how much I like your picture and how generous it is of you to give it me. If I try I shall probably say the wrong things, but its meticulous melancholy speaks straight to me; it seems more than Stoneferry, more than Hull; it's well, I was about to say life itself, but that would be overdoing it; it's very much life as *I* see it, anyway. I love the sky, and the railings, and the rising line of the path behind them. What you say about it – that this was a farm – adds to the, I'm afraid, literary interest for me. I have a little 19th century water-coloured print of a Russian village where Napoleon stopped before the battle of Borodino, which I like for much the same reasons, but yours is much better. A painter, Humphrey Ocean, currently painting my picture for the Nat. Portrait Gallery, likes it too.

How I wish there could be a Tarling exhibition, so that I could see them all.

I've been wondering if your giddy spells are improving. Such things are very worrying – I've started to get them on *public* occasions, which of course is inconvenient; my (not v. good) doctor says it's stage fright! But why now, after all these years? Anyway, it gives me an excuse to avoid them. I hope there's a similar silver lining for you. Once again, thanks.

Yours ever, Philip.

Philip's declared preference was for paintings which showed a faithful reproduction of nature; he liked pictures which showed life as it is rather than life as it isn't: a stance which is consistent with his predilection for naturalism and clarity rather than artifice in works of literature. A browse through the *Oxford Book of Twentieth-Century English Verse* confirms his partiality for work which has this kind of accessibility and, indeed, it is one of the main things for which his detractors criticize him. When the book came out many of the reviewers considered his choice eccentric and too wide-ranging. They deplored his exclusion of the 'difficult' in favour of work which had a strong narrative thread.

His next letter shows his growing nervousness about venturing out in the evenings. Round about this time he came to my house to dinner and although he had been many times before, the parking bothered him and he got confused. I had reminded him on the telephone that mine was the eunuch house, the first one without balls (out of a row of six houses with decorative stone globes on their gateposts, mine were missing), but he approached the row from the opposite direction, shot right past the house and arrived feeling flustered. That such trifles should upset him so is, I think, indicative of the frail state of his health at that time.

1st January, 1985.

Dear Ted,

Thank you for your letter and card before Christmas. You wrote very kindly, and I am ashamed of not having responded earlier. In fact, I don't think I have been well during the whole holiday (of which this is the last day); awful fits of anxiety and depression together with general lack of appetite and listlessness. No doubt there is a virus that produces such a condition, though contemplation of life as it is offered me does it just as well. Monica hasn't been well either.

Hence the prospect of an unannounced visit to you seemed too daunting in my enfeebled condition, though

197

I should love to see the paintings and congratulate you on achieving them. Which side is No. 17? Is it possible to park outside? Do I ring a bell? Since now WORK is restarting I am really only free in the evenings, is it possible to look at paintings in artificial light? You will think I am making difficulties but the least obstacle tends to throw me at present.

You mention George H, I had a euphoric letter from him and his Christmas card included a photograph of his son Aaron when five *days* old. Since I find babies nauseating that left me cold. I should hazard that G. is a very happy man, or at least is anxious to impress on me that this is the case. He hasn't changed much in appearance, at least when I saw him 2½ years ago. He must be 50 now, surely?

Talking of Hull luminaries, I was hailed by —— the other day who told me he was taking early retirement (whatever from?) and going to work in the Egyptology Department of the British Museum, heaven knows as what. One of the surly men in buttons who make you feel your flies are undone, perhaps. I thought they were all tried and trusted ex-service-men. I can't imagine —— lasting long.

Your letter sounded fairly cheerful, which gladdened me: I hope 1985 brings you all sorts of unexpected blessings and plenty of good luck. I look forward to seeing you and the paintings.

Yours ever, Philip.

Philip finally did make his promised visit, against which Ted (himself not much of a drinker) had laid in a bottle of whisky. Philip brought one too and, though he diluted his drink with water, they consumed the best part of both bottles during the long evening. Philip was interested in a cartoon drawing, by Ern Shaw, of Ted's father who had been a well-known local boxer. He talked animatedly about his love of the sport and danced round the room describing defences and attacks he would have made in various famous bouts. Ted tried to photograph him in one of these poses but by the time he had fiddled with camera adjustments, Philip's arms were halfway down and the resulting snap shows him, under the 200-watt bulb, looking like an orang-utang.

Ted had described 17 Pearson Avenue as looking like something Gustave Doré might have designed on his deathbed, but Philip liked the house and the attic flat. He said that he himself had always lived at the top of buildings (this is not quite true) and that it pleased him to do so. He went round the room systematically looking at the books, the pictures, the records and commenting on them. As far as poetry went he did not read new stuff, just went back to his old favourites, and he noted with approval the volumes of Sassoon, Edward Thomas and Hardy. He spotted Wodehouse's *Over Seventy* and said he hadn't read it. He had heard Wodehouse was a bit of a bastard. Would he like to borrow it? No, he would get hold of a copy himself. Later, when Ted was showing him an early edition of *Wessex Poems*, he mentioned a Hardy poem from *Winter Words*, the title of which he couldn't remember, the one about Mrs Masters, whereupon Philip said this was 'The Lodging-House Fuchsias' and proceeded to recite it beautifully from memory. Ted says he made it sound so fresh and true, it might have been written that day by Larkin.

He admired Ted's sensuous drawings of a number of his past girlfriends one of whom, a practical, domesticated girl, when she had heard of Napoleon's message to Josephine *don't wash, I'm coming home*, had concluded that the emperor, on his return, wouldn't care to see heaps of ironing about the place. Philip also admired a reproduction of Nicholas Hilliard's portrait of a gentleman among roses (Ted explained that his *Wild Whistle* cover photograph was a visual pun on this picture) and Ted's painting of Albert Dock (the entrance to which has been demolished). Philip liked the latter so much that Ted gave it to him.

The whisky flowed and the hours passed but Ted says he remembers chiefly inconsequential details such as the fact that, for lack of a more suitable vessel, he was reduced to serving the water for Philip's whisky in a Northern Dairies milk bottle. Philip reminisced about his early days in Hull and his visits to me and George in Hessle. After saying that he felt perplexed by the divorce, he talked of meeting my rival, the young woman George brought to our house, and of feeling at the time that I was being mistreated. But then he disclaimed, 'I was very much on the sidelines.' This is the characteristic position Philip saw himself as occupying and I think it was one he consciously chose and desired to keep.

He complained of his bad health and, seemingly by a stream of association, of how upset he felt that Marvell had not collaborated in the projected publication of a Larkin Selected Poems. It was no doubt in his mind that most well known poets have the luck to see their Selected Poems if not their Collected Poems published before they die. He did, however, say he received a goodly annual sum from his 50% profit-sharing contract on *The Less Deceived*. Another satisfaction was the letter Mrs Thatcher had sent him saying how sorry she was that he did not feel inclined to accept the Poet Laureateship.

The talk turned inevitably to his own inability to write poetry. 'I can't do it. I just can't do it', he said, in some anguish. Ted, at a loss to find the right words of comfort (if there are any), offered the feeble consolation that at least he would be spared any further hard work. Philip stared solemnly into the carpet and answered that he had enjoyed every minute of it.

His last letter to Ted is full of his usual forebodings, but he must have known much that he left unsaid.

29th March, 1985.

. . . The Albert Dock is a lamentable record, making me doubly glad to have the picture. And I don't come out

200

too badly, holding it: can't do anything about my chin, but I suppose it plays its part in balancing the curious mass of my head.

I ought to have written to thank you for the evening we had, and to apologise for giving you the trouble of returning the photo-portrait [the Humphrey Ocean one] I'm sorry. Feb. and March have been full of medical worries of one sort or another: nothing serious (I hope), but not out of the wood yet. Cut down on drink is the main edict, but they are itching to get down my throat and up my arse just to keep in practice. It's all very depressing. I suppose the rest of my life will be more or less like this.

And isn't the weather foul! Thank God I haven't to go anywhere. Most of my colleagues are off at conferences. I hope Cambridge [Ted was about to visit his sister there] is less bleak than everywhere seems to be.

I found [Douglas Dunn's] *Elegies* difficult to comment on apart from saying how it brought it all back, even to people very much on the sidelines such as myself. I don't mean they are not good poems, just that it's so hard to distance oneself far enough to be able to think in such terms.

My ex-secretary has drawn 1st and 2nd favourites in the Grand National draw at her Golf Club. So not everyone is unhappy.

Yours ever, Philip.

Philip did not live to see Ted's latest production, a collection of thirty-six poems by Frank Redpath called *To the Village*, with an introduction by Douglas Dunn, a very worthy successor to Joan Barton's *The Mistress*. It came out in June 1986 although it had been almost a year in preparation. Ted began printing it in the February of 1986. He felt depressed by the fact that he was too hard up to buy new founts of type for the Adana and that the impression was not going to be as sharp as he would have liked. Once he had started setting up the poems he became so absorbed in the job that he put these thoughts aside and editorial rigour took over. At all hours of the day and night he would telephone Frank with questions such as: 'Don't you think we need a semi-colon before the last clause in the penultimate line of the first stanza of . . . ?'

Four years earlier, in 1982, Bloodaxe had published an anthology entitled *A Rumoured City: New Poets from Hull* edited by Douglas Dunn. Frank was by far the oldest of the ten poets represented. He had been producing a small but steady output of poems since the 1940s but, until *Wave* came, he had only once been able to bring himself to seek publication. To coincide with the launching of *A Rumoured City*, the poets were invited to take part in a public reading at the University. Philip, who had written the book's Foreword, greeted Frank before the reading with: 'For God's sake come and talk to me. I can't talk to people who don't know who Janet Gaynor was.' Later, he confided 'Yours are the only poems in the book I would have been glad to have written.'

Frank's initial response was to feel thrilled at being complimented by a poet whose work he so much admired. But the feeling changed to sadness as he thought of the words Philip had used, with their implication of increasing isolation from the work of the younger poets coupled with a wistful lament for a fulfilment which he was hardly ever again to enjoy.

Twenty

Ted and I went to see Philip at the Nuffield nursing home on 18 July 1985. Monica had asked me not to take him anything. 'Not a flower or a plant?' I asked 'No. His room is too small and he'll only worry about what to do with it.' I felt anxious during the ten minutes we waited in the reception area, not knowing how ill Philip would be. We were led through corridors to his room, compact and neat, with easy-to-clean, built-in, chipboard fitments. To my relief, he was sitting in a chair next to his bed, looking out at the view, wearing a smart, light grey, summer jacket, dark grey trousers and maroon leather slippers. He told us that he was going home the next day; all the doctors told him he was ready to go although he himself was uneasy about it: 'I can dress myself and go to the lavatory but not much more than that and I dread having to try to cope with the ordinary things such as getting out of the bath, driving the car, going into shops, banks, etc. Thank God I've got arms; my legs are useless.' For a while we talked about such trivia as the weather then, although Ted and I had agreed beforehand not to tell him about our own troubles, we somehow found ourselves talking about my cystitis and Ted's high blood-pressure.

Philip told us he had been ill since Christmas and, six weeks ago, he had had part of his oesophagus removed at the Hull Royal Infirmary and had then transferred to the Nuffield to recuperate. A few days later he vomited after eating his lunch; the vomit got into his lungs and he collapsed. Luckily a nurse found him. They took him back to the Infirmary and put him into an intensive care unit. He was unconscious for five days. 'The first thing I remember is coming to with some bugger kneeling on me and telling me when to breathe in and out.' He was full of praise for the hospital but found it terribly noisy and could not sleep. Always a fitful sleeper, he averaged about five hours a night. 'At least at the Nuffield, if I wake at two o'clock I can ring the bell and ask the nurse for a cup of tea. *Should* be able to at a hundred and fifty pounds a day. I joined BUPA years ago, thank God.'

I asked if the food was good and he said that on the whole it was not bad. He had had a meal a few days earlier. It looked promising on the menu – Seafood Surprise – and he thought it would be scampi on rice. 'I got the rice all right but instead of prawns there was tinned salmon and green peppers.' He pulled an inimitable wry face. 'Not long afterwards I rushed off and produced this absolutely pure diarrhoea. It squirted out of me like water from a fire hose. I lost all the nourishment.'

Ted tried to steer the conversation into related, but slightly less gloomy, channels by asking Philip if 'How' – a poem that begins with a brief description of Hull Royal Infirmary – was a first attempt at the hospital theme and if it pre-dated 'The Building' included in *High Windows*. Philip said that he could not remember and would need to look at his notebooks. The poem starts:

> How high they build hospitals!
> Lighted cliffs, against dawns
> Of days people will die on.

He was worried about having to go to London in November to receive his Companion of Honour award from the Queen. His legs had lost all their power and he found it very difficult to climb stairs. He asked Ted what he was doing to pass the time and expressed interest when Ted told him that he was about to begin to print Frank Redpath's book of poems, *To the Village*.

On our way home, Ted said to me that while they talked about Frank's book he was remembering a long conversation he had had with Philip some years earlier. In it he mentioned to Philip that Joan Barton had received a letter from C. Day Lewis only days before his death. (I read this letter recently and, knowing all the circumstances, was most moved by it. Day Lewis opened by saying that he hoped Joan would not mind being written to by a total stranger, but that he wanted her to know how much he had enjoyed reading *The Mistress*, particularly the title poem, 'Thoughts at Happisburgh', 'Rain in a Summer Night' and 'The Virgin with The Bread and Milk'. He told her that his wife, Jill Balcon, was writing the letter for him as he was not well enough to do it himself, but that he wanted to assure Joan of what great pleasure some of her poems had already given him.) Philip said he had given Day Lewis a copy of the book during a visit to *The Lemons*, Kingsley Amis's home at the time, when Day Lewis was obviously close to death. Philip was surprised that at such a time the man was still showing a keen interest in poets and poetry. He fancied that when his own time came the arts would be far from his thoughts; those would be fixed on the main event. These remarks were at the back of Ted's mind, whereas I think I was unwilling to face the possibility that Philip might be dying. The fact that he had survived so much major surgery and a five-day coma, yet was still the same old Philip, persuaded me – what I wanted to believe – that he still had some years of life ahead of him.

Although I had seen Philip regularly over the years, he had not seen much of my daughters, so I showed him some recent photographs. He thought Laurien looked authoritative and mature. I told him school-teaching does that to you – makes you bossy. He said he would not have recognized Alison who now looked long and thin like me.

He remembered her, from ten years earlier, as being square-faced, dark-skinned and looking just like her father. I had brought the photographs to show him because I did not know what state he would be in and I feared that he might not be up to talking very much. He kept up conversation for over an hour – waving away a nurse who came to indicate our time was up – but much of what he said was sad and fearful: 'I feel I've passed a barrier. I've moved from middle age to old age and from reasonable health to all the awful things that can happen to you.' He was worried about his cough which the doctors dismissed, and he felt that he would not live long. I told him (and believed) that it was normal to feel this sort of post-operation depression. My mind went back to an earlier conversation when worries about his eventual retirement had constantly cropped up, brought on no doubt by the fact that Betty, his secretary, was due to retire in 1984. What would he do, being a man with no hobbies (he brought the word out with a mixture of regret and derision); what would there be to look forward to but stagnation and death? On that occasion I had suggested yoga, swimming, painting and walking – my own devices for staving off senility – to which he replied, 'Oh God, I'm so unfit.'

After tea and biscuits, he brightened up and complained to us about the inordinate number of shirts the library porters were asking for. A porter talking to him about changed standards of cleanliness, had said to him, 'Men used to bath once a week and wear seven clean shirts, now they bath seven times a week and wear one.' He also quoted an Oxford don who had said of the students, 'Baths! What do they want with baths? They're only here for eight weeks.'

It was a beautiful, sunny day and he asked us to walk round the garden with him – two or three perambulations a day were what the doctor ordered. We offered him our arms to lean on but he said he could manage better on his own. He was slow but did not seem to be in pain. As we walked down a path edged with lupins, delphiniums and rose-bushes, Philip spoke about jazz to Ted whose indifference to it had, in the last ten years, become an aversion. He mentioned this to Philip more than once during that time but he seemed not to believe him. Philip said that Michael Bowen had told him that Mike Daniels had started playing again. Did Ted remember him? Ted said that he did and went on to recite a string of names of musicians he had once played in bands with, who had now faded from the music scene. 'What are they all doing now?' 'Clerical jobs?' mused Philip. 'More likely session work for pop stars', I hazarded. 'Claiming Supplementary Benefit seems *much* more likely', said Ted.

Back in his bedroom, he said he had been a callous bastard over other people's illnesses. 'Hadn't realized. Failure of imagination.' He then spoke of a mutual acquaintance who had recently died: 'I think she came from a good border family.' I pondered his use of the word 'good'. To him it represented class and status whereas for me it meant honest and kind. Philip was no snob; his natural friendliness and tact rendered social class irrelevant most of the time but occasionally it did impose a barrier. I felt this when we were talking about bathing. I had mentioned our weekly bath ritual of the tin tub in front of the fire, when status was indicated by the dunking order: Dad, Mum, Harry, then me. Philip had pulled a face expressing distaste. I suppose his comfortable background had given him no understanding of the realities of working-class life and he had no wish to know about them. He met you on the level of mutual interest.

He took us to the door and when we had kissed goodbye (he was always a tenderly affectionate man) I asked if I could see him at home. He had talked to us for longer than the hospital advised and he now looked frail and tired. 'Wait a few weeks until I'm feeling better', he said. Then, as we parted, he grinned and said, 'You'll be able to say you're the last people to see me alive.' The lugubriousness was typical of him but both Ted and I felt a lump in the throat. Philip must have known then that he was dying yet he maintained the myth that he only needed to re-learn the use of his limbs – 'I just don't know how I'm going to get to the off-licence.'

A few weeks later I telephoned to ask him if he would like to come to a farewell party for Alison, who was going to Botswana for two years. Philip declined the invitation, saying that he was taking things very quietly and that the most stimulating thing he had managed lately was a quiet lunch with a friend. Although subdued, he was his usual polite self, asked after Peter, and Laurien and sent his best wishes to Alison – though he could not think why she would want to go so far away, particularly to a country which might be prejudiced against whites. He told me some horror stories reported by friends. And wouldn't she have to learn the language? I told him a bit about the country and tried to be reassuring, but he was not convinced. He told me a joke, which I have forgotten, and then talked about how he was managing. Monica was looking after him well; she did the cooking and they helped each other, he said. That was the last time I spoke to him. For a few days it had been on my mind that I must telephone to swap news or perhaps arrange a Christmas get-together. Then, on the 2nd December, I switched on the radio and heard the announcement of his death.

Twenty-One

On Monday the 30th June, 1986, five hundred people gathered in The Middleton Hall to hear some twenty of Philip's friends and colleagues pay tribute to him in an evening of thanksgiving. Personal reminiscences were interspersed with readings from his prose and poems, snatches of jazz, a video glimpse into his room at the library and at home, and overhead projections of various letters and notes he had written. The Middleton Hall is not the most intimate of settings. Its pale wood and dry acoustics give it a bleak and unsympathetically functional air. But there was nothing funereal about the occasion and the laughter was loud and regular as each contributor bore testimony to Philip's most endearing gift, his sense of humour.

During the evening I became more and more struck by evidence of Philip's chameleon-like nature as disclosed by each speaker. His interests and sympathies were clearly much wider than I had thought. Perhaps this was because he gave his full attention to everyone he had dealings with. I myself never had the feeling that he was waiting for a gap in the conversation in order to inject his own views. He seemed invariably to follow one's train of thought rather than his own and, I suppose, his own interests were widened because of this. Either he had schooled himself or had a natural talent for being able to listen to others. I think the latter, for though good listeners are rare, it seems Philip was one; friends of his youth lay stress on his habitual politeness.

Ray Brett acknowledged that although Philip was unreserved with his friends, there was a private side to his nature, a 'solitude that nourished his poetry and which he guarded.' He needed, I feel, to be able to distance himself from others and from his participating self, to become the outsider, objectively observing his own motives and the life going on around him.

Since such jobs were rare and much sought after, the post of University Librarian, which Philip applied for in 1954, attracted many talented and well-qualified competitors. Still young for the job, and relatively unknown, Philip was not, on paper at least, the favoured applicant. But Ray, who was then chairman of the Library Committee, remembered how Philip had impressed them all with 'his quiet modesty, his humour, his wit, his intelligence and his genuineness.' Ray's statement that there was about Philip 'a kind of simplicity that goes with real greatness' seemed to me to be most apposite and true. It was the hallmark of his poetry, his criticism and his conversation.

Maeve Brennan's recollection mentioned the poem *Aubade* which was first published in 1977, eight years before Philip's death. She described how Philip used to come to her office at the end of the day to catch up on the day's news and of how, over a number of such visits he unfolded the whole poem to her. 'At first I did not realize he was rehearsing a new poem but it soon became clear that he had put the fears and ideas we had so often discussed into verse. The impact on me was vivid. Its awesome power recalled for me Newman's *Dream of Gerontius* to which, of course, it is a bleak contrast, uncompromising in its lack of hope. With this comment Philip did not disagree. The sad epilogue is the knowledge that during his last illness he experienced with such awful intensity the fears he expressed so vividly in this poem'. It was a sombre but fitting note on which to close the evening.

Although Philip had no religious belief he envied those

who had. Like Thomas Hardy before him, he was emotionally drawn to the liturgy and ritual of the church but his rationality would not allow him the comfort that an act of faith would have bestowed.

Philip's initial distaste for publicity moderated sufficiently over the years for him to be able to take pleasure and pride in the honours and distinctions that society gave him. He had, I am sure, a number of reasons for rejecting the Poet Laureateship. Certainly, an important one was that he felt his gift for writing poetry had at last left him. But there was no reason more potent than that in becoming Laureate he could not have avoided attracting a greater degree of publicity than he could have borne.

Philip is buried in the municipal graveyard in Cottingham. Around him lie an assortment of locals but, as far as I could see, no losels or loblolly-men. There are lots of gipsies nearby and one of them, Whacker Smith, has a grand, black, ornately-carved memorial stone. In contrast stands Philip's headstone, small, plain and featuring only his name, dates and the designation – writer.

A month after the Middleton Hall Memorial evening, Peter and I flew to Botswana for six weeks to stay with Alison in Serowe where she was teaching. It was the first time I had flown and such an opportunity was unlikely to occur again. There is one tarmac road which runs through Botswana between South Africa and Zimbabwe; Serowe lies to the west at the end of a forty kilometre adjoining road. It is a large isolated village on the edge of the Kalahari and it spreads over two hillsides. Its red earth is dotted with rondavels – round huts made of wooden stakes, plastered with mud and topped with reed thatch – and a sprinkling of mostly single-storey breeze-block houses with corrugated iron roofs. There are virtually no telephones, no numbers on doors, no streets and no public transport.

Sitting on the verandah of Alison's bungalow I listened

to the soft Setswana voices of the passing school-children, saw donkey carts pass laden with thorny trees to be sold to those people lucky enough to have a donkey-boiler to heat their water, and watched a locust lay its hundreds of eggs in the rubber-tree hedge that surrounded the dirt yard. Cows and goats came and nibbled any vestige of leaf or kitchen waste and the latter would even eat cardboard boxes if nothing better was offered. After a couple of weeks of saying 'It's a lovely day today', I realized that it was always going to be a lovely day and that the weather, unless rain promised – and there were months to go before the rainy season – was not a relevant topic of conversation. From Hull to Serowe was a most dramatic change of air.

When Alison's school term finished, we headed north in her ancient Volkswagen Beetle and saw sights undreamed of. We drove down hundreds of arrow-straight kilometres of deserted road with nothing but red, gold and green bush on each side as far as the eye could see. Occasionally a file of women would appear carrying stooks of thatch on their heads and often a baby on their backs, their erect carriage and patient faces showing no sign of strain at the burdens they bore. By the side of the Chobe and Zambesi rivers we cowered under the gaze of a herd of elephants, were amused by the delicate amblings of the giraffes and amazed at how toylike and newly painted the shy zebras looked.

The space and time I found in Africa gave me a chance to take stock of my life. I had written most of this memoir during the weeks before leaving England: the writing of it had brought me close enough to Philip's life to be able to see the pattern and direction of it and, in some way, this enabled me to discern the shape of my own life. The sort of background I come from does not encourage this kind of introspection: life is simple, real, and every day brings its accustomed tasks. Life is something you just get on with. Therefore it was novel for me to feel that my life warranted anything so portentous as analysis.

I realized that I was glad to be drawing towards the end

of my teaching career and that I felt completely out of sympathy with the prevailing ethos in education today. The entrepreneurial approach is distasteful to me. The tailoring of education to fit the dictates of market forces (though sociologists would maintain that this has always been the case) is alien to all that I have ever believed in and worked for. Insubstantial little courses in which subjects are so watered down as to become unrecognizable are totally unsatisfying to the teacher and useless to the taught. Taking early retirement has its risks of course. There is something highly seductive about a regular salary. It does not even need to approach the national average to make you delude yourself that what you are doing is worthwhile. The material comforts that the salary brings encourage the belief that there is some deep meaning in the impenetrable jargon and proliferating sets of initials so beloved of the highly paid management teams who are very far removed from the process of teaching. Elbowed by uncaring young superiors who see a woman over 50 as a dispensable item, and feeling so out of step with the times, I realized it was time to go.

AFTERWORD

In the last few years Philip Larkin's *Collected Poems* (The Marvell Press and Faber, 1988) and *Selected Letters* (Faber, 1992) have appeared. Both books have attracted a good deal of acclaim and controversy. I once met Philip in the street, shortly after the new library had opened, and he said, 'I've got a big useless present for you.' 'Is it the old library?' I quipped. He was not amused but the next day he appeared on my doorstep carrying a huge box of chocolates. I found the *Collected Poems* rather like that box of chocolates – a variety of goodies, not all of them to my taste, but with lots of unexpected delights.

I was pleased to find poems about his parents other than the much published ones. 'An April Sunday brings the Snow' is a touching elegy on his father's death and 'Mother, Summer, I,', a sympathetic evocation of his and his mother's mistrust of summer. The agony of love is well documented too, providing, as Philip might say, sentiments to which each bosom returns an echo. I am fascinated by the large unwieldy fragment of a love poem, 'The Dance', and think I can see why he dropped it. It's also possible to pick out the eighteen or so 'filler' poems he would have used if there had been another selection of poems to succeed *High Windows,* but the half dozen or so substantial ones he would have needed were never written; there is only the bleak 'Aubade'.

The publication of Anthony Thwaite's *Selected Letters of Philip Larkin* has revealed different aspects of the man in more detail than we might want to know or might feel comfortable knowing. Some of the letters are surprising, some shocking, but they are the kind of letters which were written out of a compulsive need and which have the immediacy and uninhibitedness of private conversation. But for me they reinforce my understanding of him as a determined joker. He liked to make you laugh, and presented you with the side of himself that he thought would appeal. So there are almost as many different voices here as there are correspondents.

It would be interesting to see the 'dutiful-son', represented in the thousands of letters he wrote to his mother. After his father died, and Philip moved away from home, he wrote to her every day. I can see how difficult it would have been to choose from these letters for the present selection, as it would have made it impossibly large. Perhaps some day they will be published in collected form.

Not having met Philip until he was thirty two years old, I was particularly grateful to learn something of his adolescence through the letters he wrote to his friend, Jim Sutton. About seventy of these are printed in the *Selected Letters* out of the two hundred or so that are deposited in the Brynmor Jones Library where I first read them. The correspondence began when Philip was sixteen and ended when he was twenty eight.

His early poems, unlike his mature work, reflect little of the stuff of his day-to-day life. It is good to know something about him before he went to Oxford, when sexual recreation was 'a socially remote thing like baccarat or clog dancing', when he could write about wanting a friend who was 'perpetually kneeling in his heart', when he was in love with D. H. Lawrence, before his father died, and before he had begun to keep quiet on the subject of his early life.

Although he professed to loathe the notion of the artist shutting himself up in an ivory tower, he did in a sense do something similar. Apart from attending to the demands of his job, and cultivating a few friends and lovers, the rest of the world could go hang. He resented any of his leisure time not being spent on his own artistic development, and the letters show this egocentricity to have set in at an early age. The letters he wrote to Jim Sutton during the war reveal Philip's obsession with writing poetry, creative prose and letters, and show his conviction that the war was such a damned inconvenient nuisance that he seldom deigned to notice or mention it. He makes clear his annoyance that it happened during *his* formative years and that it should have tried to involve him in its violence and pointlessness. His sheer relief when he was rejected for active service on the grounds of defective eyesight, is palpable. As he matured he saw the need to adopt some protective camouflage to mask his lack of public spiritedness. It provided him with a simple surface of 'one of those old-type natural fouled-up guys' to hide behind.

I remember reading, years ago, a passage where D. H. Lawrence refers to red trousers, saying that if Englishmen were to wear them they would lose their inhibitions. Reading a letter by the nineteen-year-old Philip to Jim Sutton, I came across the following sentences, and wondered if Philip had Lawrence's advice in mind when he made his purchase. 'I have bought a pair of crimson trousers – like a red, red rose. Bloody fine. Only pair in Oxford. . . . My happiness is generally a silly sort of woman's happiness – happy because the sun is shining and because I'm wearing nice clothes and because I'm going to be famous.' I am glad to have this early image, passionate and idealistic, to hold against some of his later expressions of cynicism and disillusionment.

My original plan on retiring from teaching was to do a Ph.D. on Larkin's poetry. I had one or two good ideas but I eventually realised that I haven't an academic mind – enthusiastic yes, critical no. It is also lonely work and I can understand why the drop-out rate is so high. Very few people are temperamentally suited to such solitary beavering. I'm sure the absence of my work will be no loss to the annals of Eng. Lit. for there must be enough bright young scholars between here and Australia to keep the Larkin industry going for many years to come.

In April 1989 my daughter, Alison, gave birth to the divine Sarah – a strong-willed, comical girl brimming with imagination. She is a never-ending source of joy and delight to us. I had never felt that abstract longing for grandchildren that so many women feel, but from the moment she was born I have been able to take the sort of irresponsible pleasure in her that poverty and immaturity prevented me from taking in my own children. During the critical weeks before Sarah's birth our good and faithful friend, Frank Redpath, ferried Alison and me to the Beverley ante-natal unit, and he and I sampled the toasted teacakes and coffee in Beverley's various teashops while Alison's unborn baby was being monitored on the heart machine.

After Sarah was safely born Frank held her in his arms and said, 'I think I qualify to be her honorary grandfather.' Eighteen months later, after a long and painful struggle with cancer, Frank died. It had been three years since he retired from teaching, and in that time – he knew he wouldn't have long – he wrote the best poems of his life. Writing with an intensity he had never before been able to give to his work, the poetry emerged sure, memorable and moving. I hope it soon finds a publisher. Sadly, *To the Village* was the final publication of The Sonus Press.

So many decades had passed since Frank had first walked me home from the W.E.A. through the streets of Hull, he reciting 'Rhapsody on a Windy Night' or 'Venus will now Say a Few Words' and me marvelling over his beautiful voice and prodigious memory. I would have been fifteen at the time and he twenty-one.

Not many months before Frank's death, I visited Frank in hospital with my friend, Jill. Though physically weak, he was as keen to entertain and amuse us as ever. It was a fine day so he took us on a nature ramble through the grounds. We came to a sunken rose garden which bore sufficient resemblance to an amphitheatre for Frank to want to test its acçoustics. He sent us to the far end of it, struck a suitable dramatic pose and then, looking resplendent in his nightwear, recited the Agincourt speech from Henry V. It was an hilarious afternoon, quite unlike any other hospital visit Jill or I had made, and it proved his fine voice and his memory were as good as ever.

In October 1991 Peter and I parted. Our relationship had lasted as long as my marriage and had been infinitely happier but differences in age, temperament and interests had begun to wear holes in the fabric of our lives. After the initial grief and anger were over, we were surprised and pleased to find we both felt a liberating sense of relief at being free, and we have remained good friends.

We were however still reeling from this break and the resultant upset when, early in January 1992, my brother who had been best pal to me and to Peter died after a massive heart attack. Almost a year has passed but I still wake up sometimes howling in disbelief that he has gone – my last link with the family in which I grew up. In the middle of December, after he had been rushed away in an ambulance, I went to his house to pick up some things he had asked me to take to him in hospital. On the table were presents he had made, half of them wrapped in festive paper and addressed. For his postman, who used to fly a Spitfire during the war, he had made a model Spitfire. A milk-cart, built for another friend, was on a shelf the cat couldn't reach, and there was a beautifully turned and polished egg-cup, for a friend's grandson, with a jokey robin perched on top of it. What loving workmanship! Henry, the stray tabby Harry rescued eight years ago, waited hopefully for his companion's return while a caring neighbour fed him twice a day. After the funeral Peter and I scooped Henry into a basket and brought him to my house to stay. He is a streetwise, Hessle Road cat with a chunk missing from each ear, and I imagined that he would terrorise the refined, muesli-belt felines that roam the Avenues' gardens, but he seems to prefer dossing on duvets and knees to doing battle outdoors.

Life continues and I have made new friends who add their own warmth and value to it but their friendship is not quite the same as that which I had with the people whose history and background I shared. I miss the values old friends represented. Frank, Harry and Philip were out of tune with the times insofar as they lived small, and although they were skilled at what they did, were modest about their achievements.

Despite these absences my retirement years are very full. They have given me the leisure to develop my interest in drawing and painting. I began by attending a nightclass, when I was still teaching, and those two hours a week were both a relaxation and a revelation. For the first time in my life I looked at objects and saw them rather than simply allowing my eye to wander over them. To be able now to devote a whole day to a painting or a piece of writing is sheer bliss. I also have the luxury of pleasing myself about the people I mix with and what I wear. There is no more need to be pleasant to humbugs in authority who feel they have a licence to be rude or cruel and who can order you not to wear trousers.

I have become more self-centred, I suppose. Lack of money is geographically restricting but there are all manner of compensatory freedoms. I can stay up all night reading, painting or partying without worrying about having to make an early start in the morning. And I can spend hours larking about with Sarah, entering the magical worlds she invents, teaching her songs and dances, reading her to sleep. That pleasure is priceless.